Lord, Save Me!

"This book offers comfort and healing amid life's inevitable worries and anxieties. By weaving together scriptural truths, insightful reflection, and honest prayers, readers will rediscover Christ's promises and find solace in his enduring presence. *Lord, Save Me!* is both a plea and a pathway to experiencing Christ's consolation and the healing power of his words."

Brya Hanan
Licensed therapist and author of *Befriending Your Inner Child*

"If life was always smooth sailing, Gary Zimak would be out of a job. But we know that it isn't always smooth sailing. Some seasons in life are tougher than others, and I believe most of us have daily struggles—those nagging little doubts and pains that can build up over time. In *Lord, Save Me!* Gary helps with the many things I struggle with. And as a lover of scripture, I appreciate Gary bringing God's Word into every aspect of life."

Gus Lloyd
Host of *Seize the Day* on Sirius XM's The Catholic Channel

"In *Lord, Save Me!* Gary Zimak does what the apostle Paul commanded the earliest Christians to do: 'Encourage one another and build one another up.' No Christian writer I know of has been more dedicated than Zimak to using scripture to build up and encourage his fellow Christians, especially those who struggle with worry and mental anguish. Read *Lord, Save Me!* and be of good heart. Let this book help you gain confidence in the Lord's personal care for you every single minute."

Cy Kellett
Host of *Catholic Answers Live*

Lord, Save Me!

Prayers and Encouragement When Life Feels Hard

Gary Zimak

AVE MARIA PRESS AVE Notre Dame, Indiana

Nihil Obstat: Reverend Monsignor Michael Heintz, PhD
           Censor Librorum

Imprimatur: Most Reverend Kevin C. Rhoades
           Bishop of Fort Wayne–South Bend
           Given at Fort Wayne, Indiana, on March 20, 2025

Founded in 1865, Ave Maria Press is a ministry of the United States Province of Holy Cross.

www.avemariapress.com

Paperback: ISBN-13 978-1-64680-293-7

E-book: ISBN-13 978-1-64680-294-4

Cover image © Mironov Konstantin/Getty Images.

Cover and text design by Andy Wagoner.

Printed and bound in the United States of America.

Library of Congress Cataloging-in-Publication Data is available.

Contents

Introduction

> Peter got out of the boat and began to walk on the
> water toward Jesus. But when he saw how [strong]
> the wind was, he became frightened; and, beginning
> to sink, he cried out, "Lord, save me!" (Mt 14:29–30)

The story of Jesus walking on the water is one of the most
famous images in the New Testament. From the shore, he sees
the disciples in their boat, struggling with the waves and wind,
and walks to them across the surface of the lake. When Peter
recognizes the Lord, he asks Jesus to call him out of the boat—
and he begins to walk on the water as well.

It's all going well—until it's not. One minute Peter is miraculously walking on the water, and the next minute he is sinking
into the sea. There is nothing in the narrative to indicate that
the storm has worsened or any external changes have taken
place. The only clue we get is that Peter "saw . . . the wind,"
was afraid, and began to sink into the Sea of Galilee. At that
moment in time, the storm was more real and powerful to the
frightened fisherman than Jesus. Regaining his composure and
recalling the Lord's presence, however, Peter uttered a heartfelt
three-word prayer that would change everything. As a result
of this desperate plea, Jesus reached out and saved Peter from
certain death.

Taking a closer look at this life-changing situation, there are five key moments that stand out:

1. **Danger:** Peter realized that he was in danger.

2. **Fear:** After observing the waves, he became afraid.

3. **Helplessness:** He realized that he couldn't save himself.

4. **A Savior:** Peter recognized that Jesus was able to save him.

5. **Action:** He turned to Jesus for help.

Let's examine each of these in greater detail:

1. **Danger**: No doubt about it, Peter was in trouble. As if the raging storm wasn't bad enough, Peter left the safety of the boat and walked directly into the storm. Looking at the facts objectively, this was clearly a dangerous situation for all concerned. Because Peter was out of the boat, however, he was especially vulnerable.

2. **Fear**: When Peter saw the wind swirling around him, he became afraid. Who can blame him, right? Not only was he out in the middle of a fierce storm, but he was actually walking on the water! While the Bible doesn't point out the details of what Peter was thinking, it's entirely possible his fisherman's brain was second-guessing the decision to get out of the boat to try to do something impossible.

3. **Helplessness**: After becoming afraid, Peter began to sink into the stormy sea. The fact that he didn't attempt to climb back in the boat probably indicates that it wasn't nearby. With that option off the table, there was nothing this experienced fisherman could do to save himself. He was helpless.

4. **A Savior**: Because Peter couldn't save himself, he was in desperate need of a savior. Fortunately for him, there just happened to be one available. The Bible clearly indicates that Peter came "toward Jesus," who was then close enough to reach out his hand and pull the sinking apostle to safety.

5. **Action**: Even though Peter was unable to save himself from the dangerous storm, he wasn't completely helpless. Recognizing that the all-powerful Jesus could help him (his use of the title "Lord" is an important clue), Peter cried out, "Lord, save me!" Jesus *immediately* reached out his hand and caught him (Mt 14:31).

At one time or another, we've all been or will be in Peter's sandals. The details and severity may vary, but the basic scenario is the same. We're faced with a problem that we can't solve on our own, and we become afraid. Unlike Peter, however, we sometimes fail to recognize the power and proximity of Jesus Christ, which can cause our fear to spiral out of control. In order for us to turn to the Lord with a heartfelt and confident plea for assistance, he must become as real to us as he was to Peter.

There has never been a time in my life when I was not Catholic and a follower of Jesus Christ, but there have been many occasions when my belief in him was more theoretical than practical. At the risk of embarrassing myself, I'd go so far as to say that I've often looked at Jesus as a historical figure. Technically, I believed that he existed and performed miracles in the past, but I struggled to believe that he could do the same for me in the present. As a result, I've spent countless hours panicking instead of calling out to Jesus for help. Does this sound familiar?

Like Peter, many of us have faced situations when we were completely helpless and absolutely needed divine intervention. In order for us to remain composed and turn to the Lord for help, however, he must become as real to us as the problem we're facing. This book is designed to help you move from a theoretical believer to a confident and consistent disciple of Jesus Christ, Lord of the Universe. Whether this weakness of faith is a constant issue for you or an intermittent one, I strongly believe that this book will help you draw closer to Jesus and view him as a friend, Lord, and Savior. Through the use of Bible verses, reflections, and original prayers, we'll work on developing a stronger, lived relationship with the One who can rescue us from our storm-related fears.

As you may already know, I am no stranger to the topic of anxiety. As someone who has a tendency to be anxious, I know firsthand what it's like to be consumed with worry and hopelessness. Fortunately, I've also learned the peace that comes from a personal relationship with Jesus Christ. In addition to my own experience as a worrier who's learned to lean on Jesus for support, I've spent more than a decade helping others move from fear to faith through my speaking and writing ministry.

Through my personal and professional experience, I've been able to identify several common manifestations of storm-related anxiety, ten of which I've included in this book. The good news is that each of these unpleasant situations gives us an opportunity to turn to Jesus for help. In each instance, we'll look at logical reasons for bringing these problems to prayer, and then we'll pray about them. The categories of each chapter are broad, but they include multiple specific applications that address a wide variety of relevant situations.

Unlike many other books, *Lord, Save Me!* doesn't have to be read sequentially. Feel free to skip to those topics that are most relevant to you at the moment. The format of the book is designed for the reflections to be read and reread, as new variations of difficulties arise and fade away.

My ultimate goal for this book is that it will help Jesus become so real to you that, like Peter, you will respond to your fears by recognizing the Lord's presence and turning to him with confident faith, fully expecting your prayer to be answered—even if you have to sink into the stormy sea for a bit!

1

When You Feel Doubtful or Uncertain

At one time or another, it's common to feel doubt about the uncertainty of life. Even Christians are not exempt from this dilemma. Because faith requires a conscious decision to believe in things unseen and unverifiable by our senses, there are numerous occasions for us to doubt that God is in control. Whether it's momentary or of a longer duration, doubt can and should be addressed. As the following reflections will demonstrate, however, addressing doubt can actually lead to a stronger faith in God.

By faith Abraham obeyed when he was called to go out to a place that he was to receive as an inheritance; he went out, not knowing where he was to go. (Heb 11:8)

Before I commit to something, I like to know the details. Knowing what to expect always makes things less frightening for me. How about you?

Unfortunately, life can be challenging for those of us who like to remain in our comfort zone. Every day is filled with some degree of uncertainty. Abraham understood this as much as anyone. When God called him to leave his homeland, however, Abraham obeyed—even though he didn't know the final destination.

Unlike us, God always sees the big picture. Any challenge he allows us to experience is designed to strengthen our faith and help us reach our final destination of eternal happiness in heaven. I don't necessarily enjoy walking by faith, and Abraham probably didn't either, but he went anyway. Today, let's pray for the strength to follow Jesus, even when we don't know all the details.

Dear Jesus, I'm feeling uncertain right now. I believe that you know what's going on with my life, but I'm having difficulty trusting you in my uncertainty. I want to trust you, but it's hard to give up control. Nonetheless, I choose to place my trust in you. Please walk with me and lead me where you need me to go. As long as you know where we're going, it's good enough for me. Thank you. Amen.

When he entered the house, the blind men approached him and Jesus said to them, "Do you believe that I can do this?" "Yes, Lord," they said to him. (Mt 9:28)

Before healing two blind men, Jesus asked them a simple question. He wanted to know if they believed in his power to heal them. Their two-word answer—"Yes, Lord"—reveals the depth of their faith. They believed that Jesus had the power to cure their blindness.

What do you need Jesus to do for you today? It may be something you're already praying for, or it may be something so impossible that you haven't even considered bringing it to Jesus. As you think of that need, imagine Jesus asking you the same question he asked the blind men. How would you respond?

If we dig deep enough, most of us can come up with some intention that seems hopeless. It could be an end to world hunger, a greater respect for the sanctity of life, the healing of an illness, or the return of a loved one to the Church. Don't panic if you don't have the confidence of the blind men. Many of us don't. Instead, let's make it our prayer for today.

Dear Jesus, even though I want to believe, I have to admit that sometimes I lack confidence in your power. As I look back on your numerous miracles, I should be able to believe that you can handle this situation. Yet, for some reason I'm struggling. The blind men believed in your power to heal them, so why can't I? I think it comes down to faith. I need your help. Please increase my faith so that I can approach you with the certainty of the two blind men. Thank you, Lord. Amen.

For I, the LORD, do not change. (Mal 3:6)

Are you tired of change and uncertainty? It seems like every day we are bombarded with bad news from every direction. Depending on your source of information, you could easily draw the conclusion that the world is falling apart. This Bible verse reminds us of something we could easily forget in these uncertain times. God is still in control!

St. Teresa of Avila faced uncertainty as she worked for reform in sixteenth-century Spain, even facing opposition from the Inquisition. Still, she clung to God in prayer and shares with us this consolation: "Let nothing disturb you. Let nothing frighten you. All things are passing away: God never changes. Patience obtains all things. Whoever has God lacks nothing; God alone suffices."

No matter how crazy the world gets, we can relax because God is still the same. Sounds like good advice to me.

Dear Jesus, I've heard it said that the only thing constant in life is change. This is very unsettling for me. I need to know that, no matter how dynamic and unpredictable life can be, some degree of stability can still be found. As I reflect on what you said and accomplished, I sometimes wish I lived two thousand years ago so I could see you and hear your voice. By faith, I know that you're still the same, but it doesn't seem like it. I'm going to move forward and believe that you haven't changed, but I could use some help. Please grant me the grace to truly believe that you are as real now as you were then. Amen.

> Amen, I say to you, if you have faith and do not waver,
> not only will you do what has been done to the fig
> tree, but even if you say to this mountain, "Be lifted
> up and thrown into the sea," it will be done. (Mt 21:21)

After cursing a fig tree and causing it to die, Jesus spoke these words to his astonished disciples. It's a powerful message that is every bit as inspiring today as it was two thousand years ago. Unfortunately, it's also a message that can be taken out of context and misinterpreted.

Without knowing the details of your life, I'm certain that there were times when you prayed for something and didn't receive it. Some may say that your faith wasn't strong enough, but I disagree. According to Jesus in Matthew 17:20, it only takes faith "the size of a mustard seed" to move a mountain. The fact that you prayed illustrates that you probably have at least mustard-seed-sized faith. If that's the case, why didn't you get what you prayed for?

Jesus often used hyperbole, or exaggeration, when trying to make a point. That's what's happening here. He wanted his disciples to understand that they are praying to someone who can move mountains, cause trees to wither, or cure diseases. Just because God can do all things, however, doesn't mean that he always wants to. Sometimes it's better for us that the mountain doesn't move or the cancer isn't cured. We may not know why, but God does.

What matters most is that we learn to bring all our needs to the Lord and trust him to answer in the way that is best. While he can undoubtedly move any mountain we encounter, doing so may prevent us from learning a valuable lesson. More than anything, Jesus wants us to have faith in him and learn that he can help us to somehow get past that enormous mountain in front of us. He can do it either by moving the mountain or by helping us to climb. Leaving the choice to him is what faith is all about.

Dear Jesus, as I continue to pray for what I need, my confidence in you is beginning to fade. Why is it that my prayers sometimes appear to go unanswered? Your references to asking, receiving, and moving mountains into the sea confuse me. Maybe I'm reading too much into your words. After all, why would you give me something that isn't good for me? Rather than try to predict how you will answer my prayer, I first need to believe that nothing is impossible for you. Please grant me the grace to believe that you can do all things. Amen.

Amen, I say to you, whoever does not accept the kingdom of God like a child will not enter it. (Mk 10:15)

Most people will read these words and conclude that Jesus is speaking about heaven. He is, but there's another piece of this message that often gets missed. In his first recorded words in Mark's gospel (1:15), Jesus announces that "the kingdom of God is at hand." In other words, it's here *now*.

If we choose to enter God's kingdom, we have to surrender our lives to Jesus. This implies giving up control and trusting him, even when we don't understand everything that he's doing. Children trust without questioning, which is why Jesus uses them as an example. Unless we're willing to do the same and submit to King Jesus, we can't be a part of his kingdom.

Worry is an attempt to control the uncontrollable. It's a futile attempt to be the king of our lives. It is not possible both to worry and to submit to the kingship of Jesus at the same time. It has to be one or the other. Let's ask him to help us.

Dear Jesus, even though I claim to be your follower and call you Lord, I'm struggling with the idea of surrendering my life to you. I can do it in theory, but not always in practice. I think it comes down to control and trust. It hurts me to admit it, but it is easier for me to trust myself more than I trust you. Please increase my confidence in you so that I'm willing to trust you like a child. Thank you. Amen.

≈≈

The human heart plans the way, but the LORD directs the steps. (Prv 16:9)

At the beginning of every day, most of us have plans for what we'll accomplish. More often than not, however, something unexpected will occur and disrupt our plans. When this happens, the Lord is leading us in another direction. It may be difficult for those of us who like to be in control, but learning to accept these unplanned happenings is the secret to following God's will. It's also the secret to peace.

I used to believe that the Lord leads us by opening doors, clearing paths, and calming stormy seas. In other words, he'll make it easy for us to follow him and do his will. While that may sometimes be the case, I've learned that he often operates by doing just the opposite. Many times he has guided me by closing doors and changing my plans. By doing so, he leads me and helps me to give up control.

I may not always like this approach, but it is effective. I can be very stubborn and sometimes think I'm serving God when I'm actually serving myself. Closed doors and disrupted plans have a way of reminding me of who's in charge and who knows best. It's an important lesson to learn.

Dear Jesus, I have to admit that I don't like closed doors and disrupted plans. Once I make up my mind that I want something, I have a tendency to force it to happen. It's a good thing that you love me too much to stand by idly while I attempt to do things that aren't good for me. I understand that you are totally in control of my life. Help me to appreciate closed doors and disrupted plans as your way of guiding me down your chosen path. Ultimately, you know what's best. Thank you for caring about me. Amen.

≈

The Jews quarreled among themselves, saying, "How can this man give us [his] flesh to eat?" (Jn 6:52)

To those in the crowd, the words of Jesus didn't make sense. Eat his body? Drink his blood? How is it possible? On the night of the Last Supper, however, his words suddenly made sense when he instituted the Sacrament of the Eucharist.

Over the years, I struggled to understand why God allowed "bad" things to happen and didn't always allow "good" things to happen. At times, my frustration got the best of me and I even walked away from him. Fortunately, I've always decided to come back and give him another chance. In time, what appeared to be senseless began to make sense.

Is there something in your life that doesn't make sense? Maybe you're dealing with a difficult problem or looking at what appears to be a hopeless situation. Ask Jesus what he wants you to do or what he wants you to learn. Give him some time, though. Sometimes he doesn't reveal everything all at once. He may eventually enlighten you, or he may ask you to trust him—temporarily or permanently. Are you willing to do so?

Dear Jesus, sometimes life just doesn't make sense to me, and it can be very frustrating. I guess I have a difficult time trusting that you know best. Please grant me the grace to trust you even when I don't understand your ways. I understand in theory that your timing is perfect, but I sometimes struggle to put it into practice. Amen.

> Now draw some out, and take it to the steward of
> the feast. (Jn 2:8)

The wine had run out at the wedding feast at Cana. After instructing the servers to fill the jugs with water, Jesus commanded them to draw some out and take it to their boss. Filling the jugs with water was relatively risk-free, but this request had higher stakes. Not only could they end up looking stupid, but they could lose their jobs. Despite the risk, however, they obeyed. As a result, Jesus performed his first miracle, turning water into wine, and the wine problem was resolved.

What would have happened if these servers didn't trust Jesus enough to obey his command? I don't know, but I do know what happened because they did. Are you willing to trust Jesus as much as they did? Your trust may be the key that unlocks the miracle you need.

Dear Jesus, it's not easy for me to obey you when I don't understand. Although I can choose to trust you even when I'm afraid or skeptical, I often choose to play it safe instead. I want to become more like the servers at the wedding, but I need your help to do so. Please strengthen my will and help me to follow you even when I don't fully understand. Amen.

> Unless you people see signs and wonders, you will
> not believe. (Jn 4:48)

How do you feel about choosing to believe in Jesus when your prayers appear to go unanswered? I've been there many times, and it's always been a struggle. It may not be easy, but through faith, it's possible to push past our feelings and choose to believe that Jesus is working even when we see or feel nothing.

No matter how I feel, I can choose to believe in Jesus. Although that choice can be accompanied by fear or doubt, I can still choose to place my trust in him. While signs and wonders can certainly help my faith to grow, I don't want to be dependent on them. I want to trust Jesus by faith, but I know I'll need some help. The best way to obtain that help is through prayer.

Dear Jesus, even though I don't want to depend on signs and wonders, I often do. Please help me to believe in you by faith and not by sight. Please increase my faith and help me to believe in you, especially when I am filled with doubt or fear. Amen.

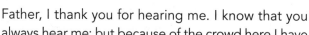

> Father, I thank you for hearing me. I know that you
> always hear me; but because of the crowd here I have
> said this, that they may believe that you sent me. (Jn
> 11:41–42)

As Jesus prepared to raise Lazarus from the dead, he turned to his Father in prayer. Take note of the words he used and the confidence with which he prayed. It's no accident that Jesus is letting us eavesdrop as he prays.

As members of the Body of Christ, we are granted the privilege of praying in Jesus's name. Praying in that manner allows us to know with certainty that our Heavenly Father always hears our prayers, even if we don't fully believe it. When we pray in the name of Jesus, we always pray with confidence. What could be better than that?

Dear Jesus, before you raised Lazarus from the dead, you turned to your Father with complete confidence that he heard your words. Unlike yours, my prayers are often intermixed with doubts and skepticism. Sometimes it feels as if I'm just going through the motions. Please grant me the grace to pray with greater confidence, knowing that our Heavenly Father always hears my prayers and will respond in the best way at the best time. Amen.

≈

And the angel said to him in reply, "I am Gabriel, who stand before God. I was sent to speak to you and to announce to you this good news. But now you will be speechless and unable to talk until the day these things take place, because you did not believe my words, which will be fulfilled at their proper time." (Lk 1:19–20)

Even though Gabriel informed Zechariah that his prayer for a son would be answered, he refused to believe. The assurance that it would happen in the future wasn't enough. He needed to see the results in order to believe. It makes me think of the many times I've done the same thing.

Zechariah and Mary received a similar message from Gabriel, but responded in different ways. I want to believe less like Zechariah and more like Mary. The way forward is choosing to believe the Lord's promise that those who ask will receive and those who seek will find.

In the end, faith isn't about seeing. It's about choosing to believe that God is trustworthy and placing our lives in his hands. Sometimes we have to believe before we can see. We are called to choose to believe that our prayers are making a difference and our faith is growing—even if it doesn't feel like it.

Dear Jesus, you assured us that those who ask will receive and those who seek will find. Even though I don't feel any different, I believe that my desire to grow closer to you will be rewarded. Thank you for your faithfulness, Lord. Maybe the fact that I'm still praying is the answer to my prayers. Amen.

≈

We have this confidence in him, that if we ask anything according to his will, he hears us. And if we know that he hears us in regard to whatever we ask, we know that what we have asked him for is ours. (1 Jn 5:14–15)

This is one of the most comforting, yet frustrating, passages in the Bible—I encourage you to spend some time thinking about it today. It doesn't mean that you will always receive the physical healing or financial blessing you're praying for. It also doesn't mean that your request will be granted immediately. It means that your prayer will always be answered in the best possible way at the best possible time.

Learning to accept this challenging concept will give you great peace, but doing so requires humility, faith, and flexibility. God wants us to be happy—not just in this life, but for all eternity. Sometimes that requires him to answer our prayers with a "no" or "not yet." I can choose to trust God, or I can choose to trust myself. Only one choice will bring me lasting peace and happiness.

Dear Jesus, I know the importance of walking by faith and not by sight. Even though I know that faith isn't a matter of feelings, I get frustrated when I can't feel your presence or see the fruit of my prayers. I will keep asking you to increase my faith and will patiently await your response. Please grant me the grace to believe in you even when my mind is filled with uncertainty and doubt. Amen.

2

When You Are Afraid

Fear is a powerful emotion. While it's technically nothing more than a feeling, it can often cause us to turn away from the Lord and his plan for our lives. In order to remind us of the potentially negative effects of fear, the message "Be not afraid" appears hundreds of times in the Bible. It's important to remember, however, that the emotion of fear can serve an important purpose in our lives. In addition to alerting us to potential danger and giving us the chance to take appropriate action, fear can remind us of how much we need God. Each time we're afraid is a new opportunity to place our trust in Jesus.

When I am afraid, in you I place my trust. (Ps 56:4)

Sometimes we look at fear and trust as being mutually exclusive. We think that it's not possible to trust God when we're afraid. This verse totally blows that theory to smithereens and reminds us that *trust is a choice* and not a feeling.

When Peter tried walking on the water and focused on the storm around him (Mt 14:30), he became afraid and began to sink. Even though he was panicking, however, he cried out to

Jesus with a prayer we should all commit to memory: "Lord, save me!"

Jesus responded instantly (Mt 14:31) by reaching out and catching him. Wow! Pretty impressive results for a three-word prayer, right?

Now, here's the lesson for us: Even though Peter was afraid, he *chose* to trust Jesus and cry out for help. Jesus responded immediately and saved him. We should follow his example and do the same, *even when we're afraid*!

Dear Jesus, even though I don't enjoy being afraid, I'm starting to realize that it's not necessarily a bad thing. The fact that I'm afraid reminds me that I need you and gives me a chance to ask for your help. Sometimes I feel bad for those who go through life without experiencing any anxiety. As a result, they never realize how great it can be to have a relationship with you. Thank you for letting me be afraid, Lord. More importantly, thank you for never leaving my side. I need you, Jesus. Amen.

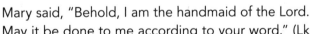

Mary said, "Behold, I am the handmaid of the Lord. May it be done to me according to your word." (Lk 1:38)

This is how Mary responded when told that she had been chosen to deliver the Messiah by a pregnancy that would come about through the power of the Holy Spirit. She received no other instructions or details, but responded with an unqualified yes.

Gabriel greeted Mary by saying, "Do not be afraid" for a reason—the Bible tells us that Mary was *greatly troubled* (Lk 1:29). But that was before she was made aware of her mission. Once she was informed of God's plan, there was no further indication that Mary was afraid. That's because of her strong faith and ability to trust God even when faced with a serious lack of details.

It's important to acknowledge and commend Mary for her strong faith, but we shouldn't stop there. Not only should she be commended, but imitated. Even if we never reach Mary's level of faith, we can certainly get closer than we are now. No matter how afraid we may be, we can always choose to trust in God's plan.

Dear Blessed Mother, thank you for saying yes and delivering our Savior. Your trust in God is amazing. I'd like to be able to trust him as much as you did, and I could really use your help. Please pray for me so that I will trust him more than I do today. Thank you, Mary. Amen.

≈

Be strong, do not fear!
Here is your God,
he comes with vindication;
With divine recompense
he comes to save you. (Is 35:4)

In this verse, the prophet Isaiah reminds us of one of the major benefits flowing from the arrival of the Messiah. Although

Jesus was born primarily to liberate us from our sins, he also came to free us from excess fear and worry. As we strive to grow closer to him and surrender to his will, we can also look forward to the greater peace that he will bring.

As someone who is intimately familiar with the emotion of fear, I find this message to be extremely comforting and very relevant. Rarely do I experience a day when I'm not afraid of something—the uncertain future, my personal weaknesses, the struggle to become holy, Satan's temptations, the reality of suffering, and many other things.

Many things in life can frighten us, but we know that God doesn't want us to be afraid. He sent Jesus into the world to save us from our sins and our fears. Even though we already know this, we need to hear it again and again.

Lord Jesus, Prince of Peace, sometimes life seems like one burden after another. With so many things to worry about, I often feel overwhelmed. As I strive to know you better, I look forward to the increased peace that you will bring. Please continue to fill me with hope, and grant me the grace to continue moving closer to you. Amen.

Peace I leave with you; my peace I give to you. Not as the world gives do I give to you. Let not your hearts be troubled or afraid. (Jn 14:27)

According to the "wisdom" of the world, peace is defined as the absence of conflict. It's hardly a spoiler alert when I tell you that this will never happen. In our fallen world, we will always face challenges and difficulties. There will never be a shortage of reasons to become overwhelmed or afraid. In the midst of this harsh reality, Jesus offers us the gift of his unique and supernatural peace.

I especially like the fact that the Lord acknowledges the difference between his peace and the world's peace. Additionally, I also appreciate his use of the word *let*. By using this verb, he reminds us that we have control over our troubled and fear-filled hearts. We do this by turning to him and accepting the gift of peace.

I strongly encourage you to take Jesus up on his offer. Ask him for that special peace only he can give. Get into the habit of asking often, and don't be afraid to remind him of his promise. He left us these words for a reason. Whenever we lack peace, it's time to ask Jesus to give us some of his. He will never turn us away empty-handed.

Dear Jesus, thank you for offering to give me your supernatural peace. I'm grateful for the reminder that lasting peace can only come from you. In a world filled with turmoil and conflict, it's comforting to know that I can still experience peace. As I spend this time with you in prayer, I gladly accept your gift of peace. Thank you for the gift and the reminder, Lord. I really need it today. Amen.

≈

Have no anxiety about anything, but in everything by prayer and petition, with thanksgiving, make your requests known to God. Then the peace of God that surpasses all understanding will guard your hearts and minds in Christ Jesus. (Phil 4:6–7)

If I had to compile a list of my go-to Bible verses for dealing with anxiety, this one would definitely make the list. In addition to telling us what we *shouldn't* do, Paul informs us of what we *should* do. Instead of giving in to our anxiety, we should turn to the Lord in prayer and ask for his help. Furthermore, Paul informs us of what will result: peace.

I can't promise that following Paul's advice will immediately make you *feel* peaceful. Sometimes it won't. Feelings come and go. True peace is more than a feeling. It is a state of mind. It is possible to be *at* peace, but not *feel* peaceful.

By choosing to pray instead of worry, however, you will be doing God's will. That reason alone should be enough for you to give it a try. Why? First, because fitting into God's design should be our main goal in life. Second, because following God's will always results in greater peace of mind—maybe not instantly, but eventually.

Dear Jesus, even though I've gotten used to responding to fear by worrying, I'm choosing today to follow Paul's advice and turn to you instead. Please help me with those issues that are causing me to be anxious. I know that you are more powerful than any of my problems, even those that appear to be unsolvable.

As I turn to you in prayer, I believe that you will help me. While maybe my belief is not as strong as my present feeling of fear, I recognize that belief is the beginning of the peace promised by Paul. Thank you, Jesus. Amen.

$$\approx$$

Do not let your hearts be troubled. (Jn 14:1)

We touched on these words earlier in the chapter, but I felt they were worth revisiting. This command is so important that Jesus repeated it multiple times in the fourteenth chapter of John's gospel. I like this verse so much that I use it as the theme of my daily email reflections. It's a message our troubled world and our troubled hearts need to hear on a daily basis.

As important as the Lord's message is, there's a message within the message that I feel may be equally important. While we should definitely work at doing what we can to "not let our hearts be troubled," we should also focus on a secondary message that we can find buried in his words: It *is* possible for us to follow his command.

It sounds difficult, but Jesus wouldn't ask us to do something that isn't possible. You may not be able to remove all anxiety from your life, but you can make the conscious decision to turn to the One who can. In time, you'll find your confidence in him increasing and your fear decreasing.

Dear Jesus, thank you for reminding me that it is possible to "not let my heart be troubled." Worrying has become such a habit for me that I've lost sight of the fact that it doesn't have to be that

*way. I know you would never ask me to do the impossible, Lord.
I also know that I can't do this on my own. Therefore, I turn to
you and ask for your help. Please fill me with your supernatural
peace that surpasses all understanding. Amen.*

> But the word of the LORD came to him: Why are you
> here, Elijah? (1 Kgs 19:9)

When Jezebel threatened to kill the prophet Elijah, he was
afraid and ran for his life. He ended up hiding in a cave, a
self-imposed prison. The Lord sought him out and asked a
simple question: "Why are you here?"

Elijah was afraid because Jezebel threatened to kill him.
He had just slain 450 false prophets, but ran for his life because
of one woman's words. Wow. Somehow, he forgot about how
the Lord came through for him in the battle of the prophets.

The evil one often plays the role of Jezebel and bombards
us with an endless assortment of threats:

"God can't help you with your problem."

"You're a loser, and you can't possibly succeed."

"God doesn't love you, because you're a sinner."

"It's only a matter of time before something bad happens
to you."

Just like Elijah, we sometimes respond by trying to hide
in a cave. In an attempt to save our lives and find security, we
lock ourselves in self-made prisons. When we behave like this,
however, we are trusting in ourselves and not in God.

If you're feeling like this, let the word of the Lord speak to you as he did to Elijah: "Why are you here?"

He doesn't want you hiding in a cave. He wants you to rely on his protection, especially when you are afraid. Will you trust him?

Lord Jesus, it makes me uncomfortable to tell you this, but sometimes I don't trust you. Instead of placing my trust in you, I often choose to trust myself instead. And, once I do that, it doesn't take too long for me to become overwhelmed and worried. The world around me often frightens me, Jesus, and I respond by hiding in some sort of cave. I know this type of behavior isn't good for me, but sometimes it's easier to live in fear than to surrender my life to you. Even though I'm scared that you might ask too much of me, I will choose to come out of my cave and yield control to you. Please lead me where you need me to be. Even when I'm afraid, I really do know that you want what's best for me. Amen.

≈

> Then the angel said to her, "Do not be afraid, Mary, for you have found favor with God." (Lk 1:30)

As we discussed earlier, the Bible clearly documents that Mary was afraid. Not only does this make me feel better, but it takes away much of my guilt. Being afraid is not a sin. Because fear is an emotion, we can't just make it go away. What we can do, however, is push past our fear and choose to trust God.

Being afraid can't stop me from choosing to place my trust in God. It can certainly make it more difficult, but it can't stop me. Just like Mary, I am capable of choosing to trust even if I'm afraid.

Fear is a God-given emotion that is designed to alert me of potential danger. When the danger is real, the Lord expects me to respond to my fear by taking action and protecting myself. Most of my fear, however, is of the imaginary variety and comes from a lack of faith.

Whether our fear is imaginary or real, it can always be viewed as an opportunity to place our trust in the Lord. Mary was afraid and chose to trust God. You and I can do the same.

Dear Jesus, even though I'm feeling afraid today, I choose to trust that you know what's best for me. Please grant me the grace to be more like Mary and surrender to your will. I realize that trusting you is a choice and not a feeling. Through the intercession of the Blessed Mother, I ask that you strengthen my faith so that I don't give in to my fears. Amen.

Then he asked them, "Why are you terrified? Do you not yet have faith?" (Mk 4:40)

Reasonable question, right? Maybe, but take note of the fact that Jesus asks them why they *are* afraid (present tense) and not why they *were* afraid. In the previous verse (Mk 4:39), we read that Jesus calmed the storm. If the storm was gone, why were they still afraid?

I can't say for sure, but there's a good possibility that they feared the storm might come back. If Jesus calmed the previous storm, why didn't they trust that he could calm the next one too? Maybe that's why he questioned their lack of faith.

I have survived every one of my previous storms, but I still tend to fear the next one. Maybe I was just lucky in the past. Sooner or later, my luck is bound to run out. Do you ever feel the same way? Maybe that's why these words are in the Bible. Sometimes we need a reminder that our faith is weak. Instead of just making us feel bad, it can increase our desire to do something about it. We may not be able to increase our faith, but we can certainly pray and ask the Lord to strengthen it.

Dear Jesus, I realize that many times my fear is caused by a lack of faith. Please increase my faith and help me trust in you in the midst of the storm. As I look back over the course of my life, I recognize that you have always provided for all of my needs. Maybe you didn't give me everything I wanted, but you never promised to do that. The fact that I'm alive today proves that you love me and have given me all that I needed. Please increase my faith so that I don't doubt you in future storms. Amen.

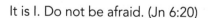

It is I. Do not be afraid. (Jn 6:20)

This message may be simple, but failing to appreciate it is the cause of much of our fear. It is a message that appears hundreds of times in the Old and New Testaments. Even though the words are familiar, it is a message that we need to hear several times each day.

Although we've heard the words many times in the past, the message is always new. That's because our circumstances change on a daily basis. Therefore, every time Jesus speaks these words and urges us not to be afraid, he does so in the midst of a totally new set of worries and challenges. One day he's commanding us not to be afraid as we deal with financial issues, and the next day he's delivering the words in the midst of a health crisis. As a result, the same words spoken in a different context take on a whole new meaning.

As you read this reflection, Jesus is urging you not to be afraid—he is reminding you that he is with you. He is bigger than whatever is causing you to be afraid. Spend some time with him now, and let his words bring you comfort. With Jesus by your side, there really is no reason to be afraid.

Dear Jesus, thank you for the encouraging message. I know that you don't want me to be afraid, but I forgot as I struggled with this current situation. When I face life's challenges, my initial request is always for you to remove the problem. I've learned that you sometimes choose another option. Instead of simply calming the storm, you often choose to accompany me and deliver the grace I need. Even though it's not always easy for me, I'll let you handle the situation. In your infinite wisdom, you really do know what's best. Amen.

≈

> When the disciples saw him walking on the sea they were terrified. "It is a ghost," they said, and they cried out in fear. (Mt 14:26)

Instead of rejoicing that the one who had previously calmed the storm just showed up, the frantic apostles cried out in fear. This same dynamic happens to us too. Sometimes our storms are so fierce that we just can't recognize the presence of Jesus. That doesn't mean he isn't with us. It just means that it's more difficult to see him than the waves that are crashing over our heads.

When the apostles failed to recognize Jesus and cried out in fear, he immediately responded with a similar message to the one we just discussed: "Take courage, it is I; do not be afraid" (Mt 14:27).

He speaks these words to you today in the midst of your storm. Don't be afraid. Why? He is with you. With his help, you'll get through it.

Dear Jesus, it's so comforting to know that you're with me in my current storm. I'm not a fan of suffering, but difficult problems always help me to remember how much I need you. Thanks for making me aware of your presence. I may be weak, but I know that you're strong. Let me know if there's anything you need me to do. Otherwise, I'll let you do the heavy lifting and deliver the peace only you can give. Amen.

≈≈

> The King of Israel, the LORD, is in your midst, you have
> no further misfortune to fear. (Zep 3:15)

In case you need to hear the message one more time, let's close out this chapter with a familiar reminder. No matter what happens to you today or in the future, Jesus is with you. He came into our world to help us, and that's why he remains with us. As long as the world continues to exist, he'll be right here with us. That makes me feel better. Hopefully, it will make you feel better too.

Jesus never promised that he would take away all our problems. What he did promise is that he will remain with us until the end of time. He is with you as you read this, and he'll be with you after you close the book and face the future. No matter what happens today, tomorrow, or in the years ahead, you can count on the presence of Jesus Christ. For that reason, there really is no need to be afraid.

Dear Jesus, thank you for coming into our world. Even though it was painful and cost you your life, you did it willingly because of your love for me. Just knowing that you're here takes away some of my fear and gives me hope about the future. With you by my side, Lord, I know we'll get through this. Amen.

3

When You Feel Weak

If you sometimes feel too weak to handle the challenges of life, you're not alone. Even St. Paul knew what weakness felt like. But instead of letting that feeling discourage him, Paul viewed it as an opportunity to let God work *through* him. I believe we can all learn something from Paul's attitude. The fact that we are weak can serve as a starting point to ask for the Lord's help. With his assistance, our weakness can be transformed into strength.

As they prayed, the place where they were gathered shook, and they were all filled with the holy Spirit and continued to speak the word of God with boldness. (Acts 4:31)

After they were released from prison for preaching the Gospel, Peter and John returned to the Church and reported what happened. They all prayed and asked God for the grace to "speak your word with all boldness" (Acts 4:29). Guess what happened? As you can see in this Bible verse, they were "filled with the holy Spirit" and spoke the "word of God with boldness"!

The fact that we receive the Holy Spirit when we are baptized doesn't mean we shouldn't pray each day to be *filled* with the Holy Spirit. That's exactly what Peter, John, and the members of the early Church did. Each day provides new opportunities for the Holy Spirit to work boldly through us. As you can see, the prayers of Peter and John were answered in a powerful way. We have every reason to believe that our prayers will be answered too.

Dear Jesus, thank you for your willingness to send us your Holy Spirit. As I deal with the challenges of this day, I'm feeling weak and overwhelmed. Reading about Peter and John's encounter with the Holy Spirit gives me confidence. Please awaken your Spirit in me so that I, too, may handle my difficulties with boldness. Amen.

Amen, amen, I say to you, whoever believes in me will do the works that I do, and will do greater ones than these, because I am going to the Father. (Jn 14:12)

Greater works than Jesus? Really? Technically, yes, this is true—but some explanation is needed.

Jesus knew that his days on earth were limited. According to God's predetermined plan, Jesus would soon ascend into heaven after accomplishing his mission on earth. Before he left, however, Jesus commissioned individuals like you and me to continue his work. With the help of the Holy Spirit, ordinary people like us have been doing that for more than two thousand years.

Not only does the power of the Holy Spirit give you the ability to love and forgive those who have hurt you, but it also enables you to experience peace in the middle of the storm. On occasion, the Lord may even perform miraculous healings through your prayers. That's what belief in Jesus can do.

Dear Jesus, it's hard to believe that someone like me can carry on your mission. I often feel too weak to handle my own responsibilities, let alone yours. Nevertheless, I believe that you were speaking the truth. Since I am incapable of handling this on my own, I'm turning to you for help. Please grant me the grace I need to do your work. Amen.

≈≈

Now go, I will assist you in speaking and teach you what you are to say. (Ex 4:12)

Over and over again, the Bible shows us that God chooses unlikely people to do his work. Moses is a case in point. Hand-picked by the Lord to lead the Israelites out of slavery, Moses felt inadequate and rattled off a list of reasons why he was not a good choice for the job:

"I'm not important enough."

"Nobody will listen to me."

"I don't know what to say."

"I'm not a good speaker."

We often find ourselves in situations that seem overwhelming: job loss, illness, death of a family member, loneliness, leadership positions, parenting, and so on. Just like Moses, we tell God that we're not qualified and that he chose the wrong person for the job. Even though we think we have made a good case, however, sometimes the problem doesn't go away. When this happens, God is responding to you with the same words he spoke to Moses: "I will help you."

You've probably heard it said that God will never give you more than you can handle. That statement is only partially true. Every day he gives us more than we can handle. The same thing applied to Moses, Mary, Joseph, the apostles, and St. Paul. They were all given more than they could handle *by themselves*. Fortunately, the Lord never asked them to handle anything by themselves. He offered to be with them and help them. He makes the same offer to each of us as well. If you're feeling stressed out, there's a good chance you're trying to do too much on your own. God would not allow you to be in the situation you're in if you *and he* couldn't handle it together. Ask him to help you today.

Lord Jesus, the fact that you came into our world shows that you care about us. With that in mind, I really need your assistance today. I am dealing with a situation much bigger than me, and I need your help. Fortunately, we can find many examples in the Bible of people like me who were overwhelmed with the challenges of life. You helped them, and I believe that you will help me. Please give me the strength I need to carry my cross. Amen.

≈

> The fruit of the Spirit is love, joy, peace, patience, kindness, generosity, faithfulness, gentleness, [and] self-control. (Gal 5:22–23)

Take a look at the list of fruits of the Holy Spirit, as described by Paul. Pretty impressive, right?

As far-fetched as it seems, you too can be filled with love, joy, peace, patience, kindness, generosity, faithfulness, gentleness, and self-control. But don't expect to get there by willpower alone or even by doing your best to imitate Jesus. The only way you will be able to bear good fruit in your life consistently is through the power of the Holy Spirit.

How exactly do you activate the power of the Spirit in your life? It's very simple. Throughout the day, make a point to invite the Holy Spirit to come alive in you. If you do that faithfully and cooperate with the grace that you receive, you will gradually see results. Keep asking and believing. It will happen.

Dear Jesus, when I look at the list of the fruits of the Holy Spirit, it sounds like a description of you and not me. I guess that's the point, right? If I allow your Spirit to work in me, I will be transformed into you! Please grant me the patience and persistence to keep asking even if I don't see immediate results. Thank you for sharing your Holy Spirit with me. Even though I feel weak, your assistance can make me strong. Amen.

≈

> Then he made his disciples get into the boat and pre-
> cede him to the other side toward Bethsaida, while
> he dismissed the crowd. (Mk 6:45)

Right after he miraculously fed the five thousand, Jesus sent
his followers ahead of him by boat while he prayed. Late that
night, the disciples got bogged down on the lake when a storm
arose—the wind and waves started battering them.

We might be alarmed that not only did Jesus send his disciples right into the storm, but he didn't even accompany them!
As the story unfolds, however, we learn that Jesus was praying
and keeping an eye on them. When the time was right, he came
near the boat by walking on the sea, but they didn't recognize
him. Hearing their frantic cries, Jesus climbed into the boat
with them, and the storm died down. Why did he allow them
to go through all of this? My guess is that he wanted them to
learn that he was more powerful than the storm.

That storm you're going through is not an accident, and
it's not a bad thing. It's an opportunity for you to trust Jesus.
Even though you can't see him, he's watching you. Instead
of panicking, turn to Jesus and ask for help. You've survived
every storm that's ever come your way. Why should this one
be any different?

*Dear Jesus, even though I can't feel your presence, I know that
you are with me in the storm. It's difficult to see you clearly as the
waves crash over the boat, but I will choose to believe that you
are with me and totally in control of the situation. Even though*

I'd like you to take away my storm, I will let you decide how to handle the matter. If you feel it best to let the storm remain, I only ask that you stay with me and fill me with your peace. In the end, that's what really matters. Amen.

Then he removed him and raised up David as their king; of him he testified, "I have found David, son of Jesse, a man after my own heart; he will carry out my every wish." (Acts 13:22)

When the Lord wasn't pleased with the actions of King Saul, he sought out "a man after his own heart" (1 Sm 13:14) and chose David as the new king. When we look at David's actions as king, though, it's not always clear how he reflects God's heart— he abuses his power by committing adultery and arranges for the murder of his beloved's husband.

Why in the world would God choose someone with so many character flaws to lead his people? Mainly because, despite the mistakes that David would make (2 Sm 11), he had a desire to "carry out God's every wish." Yes, David would mess up, but he would also acknowledge his wrongdoing and ask for forgiveness.

God is not looking for perfection. He is looking for those who desire to do his will. That's really good news for us. No matter how badly we mess up, the Lord will forgive us (and use us) if we let him. It all comes down to our desire to serve him. Let us pray that at the end of our lives God will refer to each one of us as a person "after his own heart."

Dear Jesus, if I was in your shoes, I don't think I would pick someone like me to do your work. As I think about it, however, it really says a lot about how powerful you are. You're not looking for perfection and strength; you're looking for someone who is willing to be used as your instrument. That's me, Lord. I'm willing. All I ask is that you help me by giving me what I need to complete the task. Thank you. Amen.

≈

But you will receive power when the holy Spirit comes upon you. (Acts 1:8)

According to Jesus, we receive power when the Holy Spirit comes upon us. He doesn't promise some wimpy, wishy-washy, fluffy vague force. He promises power! That means the ability to do great things in his name, including healings, prophecy, persuasive preaching, and much more. All of this happens by the power of the Holy Spirit.

It's always a good idea to recognize what we received when we were baptized and confirmed. We received power! It's up to you to pray for this power to be released every day by inviting the Holy Spirit to come alive in you. If you get in the habit of praying for it every day, the power of the Spirit will be released in you. Sometimes the results will be imperceptible, and sometimes they will be astonishing. Leave the results up to the Holy Spirit, who knows what to do and when to do it. Your job is to pray for the Holy Spirit's power to be unleashed in you.

Dear Jesus, I believe you when you promised that we will receive power through the coming of the Holy Spirit. I don't feel especially powerful right now, but I know that it's not your fault. Please awaken your Holy Spirit in me and grant me the power I need. Thank you for hearing and answering my prayer. I ask this in your name. Amen.

~~~

Peter got out of the boat and began to walk on the water toward Jesus. (Mt 14:29)

If Jesus calls you to do something, he will give you what you need to accomplish it. The task may involve a job change or a call to religious life, but it could also center on a financial crisis or unexpected illness. If he brings you to it, he will bring you through it.

The key is to imitate Peter and stay focused on Jesus. As seen in the above verse, Peter was able to do the impossible as long as he focused on the Lord. When he turned away from Jesus and looked at the storm, things started to fall apart: "But when he saw how [strong] the wind was he became frightened; and, beginning to sink, he cried out, 'Lord, save me!'" (Mt 14:30). Peter was doing a great job walking on the water until he gave all his attention to the storm. As he began to sink, however, he regained his focus and cried out to Jesus for help.

It's easy to become discouraged and afraid when you're in the middle of the storm, especially when you focus more on the problem than on the Lord. Fortunately, the solution is simple. Just like Peter, turning to Jesus is the best option. If you need help coming up with the right words, try using the same three words as Peter. The following prayer is the shortest one in the entire book, but it worked so well for Peter that I didn't want to change it.

Lord, save me! Amen.

Where can we buy enough food for them to eat? (Jn 6:5)

With five thousand men to feed and no supplies, this seems like a reasonable question until we consider that the person doing the asking is Jesus, who would shortly go on to miraculously feed all of those hungry people. Why would Jesus ask Philip such a question? Did he momentarily forget about his ability to perform a miracle?

The Bible tells us that Jesus knew what he was about to do, but asked the question to test Philip. This gives us a chance to see what Philip was thinking. He responded, "Two hundred days' wages worth of food would not be enough for each of them to have a little" (Jn 6:7), which indicates that he was focused solely on his material limitations. He never thought to ask Jesus for help.

Sound familiar? Just like Philip, we sometimes focus so much on our own limitations that we become discouraged. You may not be able to solve your problem, but that doesn't mean it's not solvable. There's always another option. His name is Jesus.

Dear Jesus, I absolutely can't figure out how to handle my current problem. I've tried everything and find myself out of options. That's why I'm turning to you. I know I should have asked for your assistance first, but I didn't. Maybe that's a good thing because I now realize how weak and powerless I am. I know you can do all things, and nothing is impossible for you. Please help me, Lord. Amen.

But the Lord stood by me and gave me strength, so that through me the proclamation might be completed and all the Gentiles might hear it. And I was rescued from the lion's mouth. (2 Tm 4:17)

Through the efforts of St. Paul, the Church flourished and many souls were led to Christ. When we look at his writings, it's obvious he knew that his success came from the Lord. It's not always a clean process, but God's will is unstoppable. No obstacle can get in the way—including our own weakness.

Keep this in mind as you deal with life's challenges today. Try not to be discouraged by bad circumstances and difficulties. God is bigger than anything you can ever face. If he wants something to happen, it will happen. His strength can make up for your weakness. Just ask Paul.

Lord Jesus, I know you would never ask me to do something impossible. Even though the problem I'm facing looks unsolvable, I know that the two of us can handle it together. Please help me as you helped Paul, and grant me the strength I need. Amen.

≈

> But Moses answered the people, "Do not fear! Stand
> your ground and see the victory the Lord will win for
> you today. For these Egyptians whom you see today
> you will never see again. The Lord will fight for you;
> you have only to keep still." Then the Lord said to
> Moses: Why are you crying out to me? Tell the Israel-
> ites to set out. (Ex 14:13–15)

As they ran from the Egyptians, Moses instructed the Israelites to stand still and wait for God to save them. The Lord then
spoke to Moses and told them to get moving!

This somewhat humorous difference of opinion reminds us
that sometimes God wants us to wait for him, but other times
he expects us to do something. Although the Lord wants to
help us with our problems, he also expects us to use our common sense and God-given gifts. In this case, the people of Israel
needed to be reminded that running away from the enemy was
the best course of action.

It's always a good idea to ask for the Lord's help with our
problems, but sometimes our ability to do something about the
situation is the answer to our prayer. Moses was right when he
told the people the Lord will fight for them and win the battle,
but he overlooked the fact that they had something to do too.
Sometimes, we're not as weak as we think we are.

*Dear Jesus, it's not always easy to figure out what you're sup-
posed to do and what I'm supposed to do. As I pray to you about
the current problems I'm facing, please let me know if you need*

me to do anything. Sometimes I feel so weak that I totally over-look my ability to do something about my situation. If you want me to act, please let me know. Amen.

≈

For when I am weak, then I am strong. (2 Cor 12:10)

Paul's words appear paradoxical on the surface, but they actually make perfect sense. Often, we need to recognize our weakness before we turn to the Lord for help.

Before getting to this point, Paul prayed in the same way I often do—by asking God to remove the problem. He actually asked God to do this not just once, but three times! He received a qualified "no" in response when God essentially told him, "I'm not going to remove your problem, *but* I'll give you the grace to handle it." This experience allowed Paul to make a profound observation: Even though he was too weak to handle the situation on his own, a little divine assistance was enough to turn weakness into strength.

That's an important lesson for those of us who feel too weak to handle what we're facing. The Lord knows our strengths and weaknesses better than we do. He would never allow us to carry an unbearable cross. While it may be too heavy for us, it's never too heavy for us *and him*.

Dear Jesus, I've asked you to take away my problem, and you've said no. I guess I'm in the same situation as St. Paul. If you're not going to remove the problem, I'll need help dealing with it. There's no way I can handle it on my own. Please grant me the grace I need to carry this heavy cross. Although I am weak, I know that you are strong. Thank you, Jesus. Amen.

4

When You
Are Discouraged

Whether it pops up suddenly or appears gradually, discouragement is a powerful emotion that can easily plunge us into hopelessness. It can be caused by many external factors, but for Christians it often boils down to a lack of faith in God's providential care. If we truly believe that God can do all things and loves us unconditionally, we should have no reason to be discouraged. Unfortunately, the fact that we have a fallen human nature and live in an imperfect world makes it difficult to avoid discouragement. The following meditations and prayers can help restore our hope and allow us to recognize the providential hand of the Lord in all events.

> Why are you downcast, my soul?
> Why do you groan within me?
> Wait for God, for I shall again praise him,
> my savior and my God. (Ps 43:5)

It's easy to become sad and discouraged when things aren't going well. But here's some good news. It doesn't have to be that way.

After you're finished reading this reflection, take a few minutes and reflect on the constant presence of God in your life: the Father, Jesus, and the Holy Spirit. Speak to them from your heart. Tell them what's bothering you. Thank the Father for creating you, and praise him for his power, love, and knowledge. Ask Jesus to help you carry your cross. Give the Holy Spirit permission to guide your emotions and inspire your thoughts, words, and actions.

Spending time with God is the best way to restore your hope and joy. It requires work on your part, but it's definitely time well spent. Give it a try today and see what happens. I guarantee it will make you feel better than watching the news or dwelling on your problems.

Dear Jesus, before I spend time reflecting on the presence of the Trinity in my life, I'd like to share a few thoughts with you. Sometimes you don't feel real to me. My problems and everything that's wrong in the world seem more real than you do. I know that it's not true, but that's how I feel. In order to break free from my discouragement, I need you to become more real to me. I'd appreciate it if you'd help me. I really want to believe that you're with me throughout the day. Please help me. Thank you. Amen.

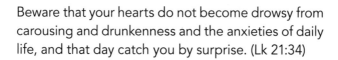

> Beware that your hearts do not become drowsy from carousing and drunkenness and the anxieties of daily life, and that day catch you by surprise. (Lk 21:34)

It's easy to get weighed down by the cares of this life. The temptation to focus on our daily struggles and problems is especially great in our information-rich age. The list of potential what-ifs has grown to a level that I have never seen before. So what can we do?

I don't recommend that you completely disconnect from what's going on in the world, but I do urge you to limit your exposure. I also encourage you to focus more on God than on your problems. Take some time each day to pray and read the Bible.

All of our earthly problems are temporary. Some last longer than others, but they will all disappear when we die (or sooner). If you spend an excessive amount of time worrying about these passing struggles, you'll waste valuable time that could be spent speaking to God and enjoying his presence.

Dear Jesus, I'm glad that you make yourself available to me at all times. As I speak to you now, I acknowledge that you love me and are more powerful than the worldly things that cause me to lose hope. Please help me to remember that nothing is impossible for you. When I look around and see nothing but bad news and a variety of potential threats, I can feel my hope slipping away. When I focus on you and all that you've accomplished and taught over the years, however, my hope begins to

grow. Help me to keep focused on the truth—that you love me
and can do all things. Amen.

> Finally, brothers, whatever is true, whatever is honorable, whatever is just, whatever is pure, whatever is lovely, whatever is gracious, if there is any excellence and if there is anything worthy of praise, think about these things. Keep on doing what you have learned and received and heard and seen in me. Then the God of peace will be with you. (Phil 4:8–9)

It might not feel like it at times, but we do have some degree of control over our thoughts. And, as St. Paul points out to the Corinthians, thinking about the right things can result in peace of mind.

One of the best ways to control your thoughts is to fill your mind with the positive message of Jesus Christ. You can do that in a number of ways: reading the Bible or other spiritual books, listening to Christian music or inspirational podcasts, watching religious TV shows, and praying.

You can also choose to binge-watch news programs, constantly scroll through your social media feed, or seek out every conspiracy theory or doomsday prediction that comes along. If you choose to go down that path, you will not find peace. It's that simple.

Several years ago, I made the decision to spend some time each day reflecting on the Good News of God's kingdom. I briefly check the news a few times daily, but that's it. More of my time is spent focusing on Jesus and his promises. And guess what? I am at peace because my mind is filled with the Good News. Don't just take my word for it, however. Listen to St. Paul. He was able to find peace in the midst of imprisonment and persecution. That's pretty amazing!

Dear Jesus, reading Paul's inspired words reminds me that I do have some degree of control over my thoughts. Choosing to expose myself to the negative, frightening, and misleading message proclaimed by the media is only going to lead to discouragement and hopelessness. Even when they present the facts, they often fail to mention the most important truth of all: You love me, and nothing in the world can happen without your permission. I'll continue to do my part by keeping my focus on your Good News. Please grant me the grace to remain firm in this practice, and fill me with the peace that can only come from you. Amen.

He said to them, "Go into the whole world and proclaim the gospel to every creature." (Mk 16:15)

It's easy to get so caught up in the division and violence taking place around us that we lose sight of the role we are each called to play in building God's kingdom. As commissioned disciples of Jesus Christ, we are expected to share the Gospel and bring peace wherever we can.

Don't think that you are unable to bring about healing and unity in the world. You can. The Gospel is a message of love and peace and needs to be preached through actions and words. Someone in your house, on social media, or in the store needs to hear or see the Good News today. Instead of complaining about what everyone else is doing or not doing, consider following the advice of Mother Teresa: "Be the one!"

Whether or not the following prayer was really composed by St. Francis doesn't matter. It's a great prayer and one that needs to be prayed. I encourage you to pray and respond to it today. Jesus is counting on you to make a difference.

Lord, make me an instrument of your peace:
where there is hatred, let me sow love;
where there is injury, pardon;
where there is doubt, faith;
where there is despair, hope;
where there is darkness, light;
where there is sadness, joy.

O divine Master, grant that I may not so much seek
to be consoled as to console,
to be understood as to understand,
to be loved as to love.
For it is in giving that we receive,
it is in pardoning that we are pardoned,
and it is in dying that we are born to eternal life.
Amen.

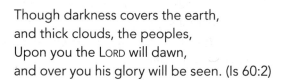

Though darkness covers the earth,
and thick clouds, the peoples,
Upon you the LORD will dawn,
and over you his glory will be seen. (Is 60:2)

Over the past few years, I've noticed a great deal of negativity and hopelessness appearing on social media. In a sense, I can understand why people feel that way. The world looks pretty dark right now.

Here's the good news. It was also dark when Jesus entered the world two thousand years ago. Did all of the darkness disappear when Jesus came on the scene? Absolutely not! But even though the darkness continued to exist, it was drowned out by the light.

As long as this world is around, the darkness will continue to exist. Even though it will be that way until the Lord comes again in glory, we have reason to hope. Remember that "the light shines in the darkness, and the darkness has not overcome it" (Jn 1:5).

Jesus came to bring us the light of his love and truth, which illuminates even the darkest parts of our lives. The secret is to spend more time focusing on the Light of the World than on the darkness.

In a way, it's like turning on the light in the middle of the night. When you flip the switch and the room is illuminated, it really doesn't matter that it's still dark outside. What matters is that you're surrounded by light.

Dear Jesus, I'm grateful that you're willing to shine your light in my world. Even though things may be dark all around me, you enable me to see clearly and avoid discouragement. Help me always to remember that you are with me. As long as that is the case, nothing will disturb me. Amen.

He must increase; I must decrease. (Jn 3:30)

It's often assumed that the ministry of John the Baptist ended once Jesus came on the scene, but that isn't true. For a period of time, both of their ministries were active. Gradually, however, John began sending his disciples to Jesus. As his words imply, this is how the plan was supposed to unfold.

Every one of us is called to decrease so that Jesus can increase in us, but it's a lifelong process. No matter how hard we try, we won't be able to think, speak, and act like Jesus overnight. As was the case with John, the decreasing and increasing process will be a gradual one.

As frustrating as it is, we must be patient with the transformation process. As long as we're trying to decrease a little and let Jesus increase a little each day, we're on the right track. Don't panic or become discouraged when you stumble. Learn to accept the fact that your imperfection can coexist with Jesus's perfection. Keep asking the Holy Spirit to work in you, and try to follow that lead. Little by little, you'll start to look less like your imperfect self and more like Jesus.

Lord Jesus, even though I try to act like you, I always seem to fail several times each day. Help me to remember that this transformation takes time and that you're looking for effort and not perfection. Thank you for being patient with me, Lord. I'll try to be more patient with myself. Amen.

Whatever place does not welcome you or listen to you, leave there and shake the dust off your feet in testimony against them. (Mk 6:11)

When trying to share our faith with others, it can be very discouraging when our message is rejected. It's painful enough when it happens once, but the pain is compounded when it happens multiple times.

When Jesus sent out the apostles, he prepared them for this situation. It's good advice for all of us. Don't keep trying to force open a locked door. Sometimes you have to walk away and look for doors that are open. You'll spare yourself a lot of aggravation and probably be more successful too.

Walking away now doesn't mean you'll never come back. It just means that you're taking a break and working elsewhere for a while. Keep praying, and give the Holy Spirit some time to work. When the time is right, that previously rejected message might be welcomed with open arms.

Dear Jesus, I'm frustrated and need some help. I'm fed up with getting rejected when I try to share you with others. I guess you know what that's like, right? Please grant me the patience I need

so that I don't give up. I can't keep going by myself, but I believe
that you will help me. Thank you, Lord. Amen.

> Simon said in reply, "Master, we have worked hard all
> night and have caught nothing, but at your command
> I will lower the nets." (Lk 5:5)

As an experienced fisherman, Simon Peter knew that it was
best to fish at night. As he learned, however, fishing during
this prime feeding time didn't guarantee success. One day,
after a bad night at sea, Peter encountered Jesus, who suggested
something bizarre. He was a carpenter, not a fisherman, yet he
instructed Peter, the lifelong expert, to go back out in broad
daylight and try again.

Even though Peter knew it was a bad idea ("We have
worked hard all night and have caught nothing"), he decided to
obey Jesus. After catching so many fish that his nets were tear-
ing, he fell at the knees of Jesus and apologized for his unbelief.

As Peter learned that day, sometimes Jesus will ask us to
do things that don't make sense. He often calls us to trust him
even when we don't understand. Jesus doesn't want us to be
irresponsible or completely disregard our common sense, but
he does expect us to step out in faith by placing our trust in
him. That may mean praying when it looks hopeless, trusting
him to provide for our needs, or believing that he'll give us the
grace to get through a difficult situation.

Just like Peter, I like to be in control. I am learning, however, that surrendering to Jesus is always the best course of

action. If you feel as if he's asking you to do something difficult, pray about it and discuss it with someone you trust. It might seem risky at first, but choosing to place your trust in Jesus is the safest thing you can do.

Dear Jesus, sometimes you ask me to do difficult things. When I try to obey you, however, it doesn't always work out. It almost seems as if you're trying to make it difficult to do your will. I don't believe that's the case, but it sometimes feels like it. I'm in that situation right now, Lord, and I'm getting frustrated. I don't need to know why things aren't working out right now, but I do need your help to keep going. Please restore my hope and grant me your peace. Amen.

Then he laid hands on his eyes a second time and he saw clearly; his sight was restored and he could see everything distinctly. (Mk 8:25)

When a blind man was brought to Jesus, Jesus touched him and asked if he could see anything. The man replied, "I see people looking like trees and walking" (Mk 8:24). After Jesus laid hands upon the man a second time, he was healed and could see.

Out of all the healing miracles performed by Jesus, this is one of my favorites. Reading through the details has often comforted me and restored my hope. This encounter reminds me that Jesus doesn't always deliver instantaneous, jaw-dropping miracles. Sometimes his miracles appear very ordinary and happen gradually.

Don't allow yourself to become discouraged or lose hope. I don't know why, but sometimes Jesus heals in stages. He has his reasons. Keep praying and believe. As this story illustrates, sometimes you just have to give Jesus a little time.

Dear Jesus, I know you didn't ask me, but I don't know why you didn't heal the blind man instantaneously. I think it would have been a more effective and powerful miracle. For some reason, however, you chose to heal this man in stages. I'm going to give you the benefit of the doubt. As you know, I'm praying for something right now, and you don't appear to be answering. This example gives me hope that sometimes your answer doesn't come instantly. I'll continue to pray and trust you. Amen.

Indeed we call blessed those who have persevered. You have heard of the perseverance of Job, and you have seen the purpose of the Lord, because "the Lord is compassionate and merciful." (Jas 5:11)

If you're trying to give up worry or a habitual sin, it's not going to happen instantly. The Holy Spirit will help you, but you'll still need to cooperate. And, because we all have a fallen human nature and tend to develop bad habits, it may take some time to see the improvement you are looking for.

Don't be surprised when you mess up. It will happen. Take comfort in the fact that the Lord has a long history of transforming imperfect creatures. He can do the same with you, as long as you don't give up.

The idea of working on this issue for the rest of your life may seem overwhelming, but what about doing it for one day? Most of us could handle giving up something or taking on something extra for one day. Why not look at life as a series of "one days" and see what happens? As the old Chinese proverb states, a journey of a thousand miles begins with a single step. Let's take that first step today and see what happens. Tomorrow will be a new day, and we can trust that Jesus will get us through that too.

Dear Jesus, I'm growing increasingly frustrated as I try to break this bad habit. It's frustrating to keep failing like this. I really should be able to get past this. Maybe you're trying to remind me of how much I need your help. Please grant me the grace and perseverance to keep working at this fault. I want to do what's right, but I can't do it without your help. Please help me. Amen.

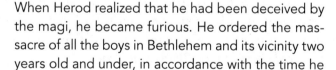

When Herod realized that he had been deceived by the magi, he became furious. He ordered the massacre of all the boys in Bethlehem and its vicinity two years old and under, in accordance with the time he had ascertained from the magi. (Mt 2:16)

As bad as the world looks today, the massacre of the Holy Innocents serves as a reminder that things were even worse two thousand years ago. In an effort to secure his position as a powerful ruler, King Herod ordered all the boys in Bethlehem two years and under to be brutally murdered. He heard the news about the newborn Messiah and wanted to eliminate the potential threat to his throne. This incident reminds us that evil and suffering will always be part of life on earth. At the same time, however, the survival of the infant Jesus proves that God's will can't be stopped.

If you feel discouraged about the current state of the world, take comfort in Herod's failure. Over the years, Herod and many others have tried unsuccessfully to eliminate Jesus and silence his message. While evil may appear to win a battle here and there, the ultimate victory belongs to the Lord. He was, is, and always will be in control. Jesus was born into this world to redeem us on the Cross and open the gates to heaven. Despite the efforts of Herod and many others to stop him, he was totally successful. So no matter how bad the defeat seems here, we can trust that, in Christ, victory is ours.

Dear Jesus, the current state of the world is extremely depressing to me. No matter where I turn, I hear bad news. My faith tells me that you're totally in control, but it sure doesn't seem like it. Please strengthen my belief in your sovereign will, and take away my discouragement. I know that you can do all things, but I need some extra help right now. Thank you. Amen.

Neither do I condemn you. Go, [and] from now on do not sin any more. (Jn 8:11)

As Jesus prepared to dismiss the woman caught in adultery, he left her with these words. The message is both comforting and challenging. While Jesus is more than willing to forgive our sins, he also expects something in return. It may sound difficult, but it really comes down to a matter of the will. What he's really looking for is not necessarily success, but desire to do better. It may prove to be difficult, but with the Lord's help, it is possible to improve.

No matter what you've done, Jesus is waiting to forgive you through the Sacrament of Confession. All he asks is that you come to him, confess your sin, ask for forgiveness, and desire not to do it again. In addition to granting you forgiveness, this great sacrament will give you the grace you need to avoid future sins.

Dear Jesus, thank you for being so merciful. At times, I get down on myself because I can't break free from sin. It almost makes me want to stop trying. I know that's not what you want me to do, however. Please grant me the grace to keep trying. I choose to believe that it's possible, but only with your help. Please help me. Amen.

5

When You Feel Lonely

Loneliness is one of the most painful emotions we can experience. Although it's a very common feeling, it's not based on reality. Even though it may feel like it at times, you are never alone. You are constantly in the presence of the Father, Son, and Holy Spirit—as well as countless angels and saints. Despite the fact that we are never truly alone, the feeling of loneliness can be very real. In this chapter, we'll look at a variety of verses, reflections, and prayers designed to lessen the feeling of loneliness that you are experiencing.

> For God so loved the world that he gave his only Son, so that everyone who believes in him might not perish but might have eternal life. (Jn 3:16)

We've seen this verse so often that we can overlook its importance. That is a *big* mistake. Unless we know how much God loves us, we will never be at peace. How can we grasp how much an invisible God loves us? We do it through Jesus!

Our Father in heaven created each of us so that we could enter into a relationship with him. That relationship is possible through Jesus, with the help of the Holy Spirit. What an amazing privilege!

No matter how you feel, *you are not alone.* Make a point to spend some time with Jesus today, and ask him to lead you to the Father. Then speak to your Father. Don't know what to say? Try using the words given to us by Jesus himself.

Dear Jesus, when your disciples asked you to teach them to pray, these are the words you gave them. Thank you for this prayer, Lord. In addition to any answers that will come from the words I'm about to pray, the fact that I'm speaking with you and about to address my Heavenly Father reminds me that I am not alone right now. Thank you.
Our Father, who art in heaven,
hallowed be thy name;
thy kingdom come,
thy will be done
on earth as it is in heaven.
Give us this day our daily bread,
and forgive us our trespasses,
as we forgive those who trespass against us;
and lead us not into temptation,
but deliver us from evil.
Amen.

≈≈

Enlarge the space for your tent,
spread out your tent cloths unsparingly;

lengthen your ropes and make firm your pegs. (Is 54:2)

If we make room for Jesus in our lives, he will gladly occupy the space. In this verse, the prophet Isaiah encourages the people to make lots of room for the Lord, knowing that God will fill up any room we prepare for him in our lives.

This dynamic is definitely something I need to remember, as I often underestimate how involved Jesus wants to be in my life. Because he respects my free will and desires, he will generally not force his way into my life. If I give him a little room, he'll occupy that little space. If I give him a great deal of room, however, he will spread out and fill up all the additional space—and bring an abundance of life with him.

Why should we be content to free up a little space for Jesus? Instead of just carving out some extra prayer time or making an effort to encounter him more deeply in church, let's make room for him in every area of our lives. If we invite Jesus into our workplace, school, or personal life, I guarantee he's going to show up. Once that happens, you'll discover the peace you've been seeking.

Dear Jesus, I'm not content just to meet you in church. Instead, I invite you to occupy all areas of my life. You are welcome in my home, in my school or workplace, and in my personal life. I'd like you to help me with all of my concerns and worries—big and small. Thank you for your willingness to get involved in the messiness of my life. I know it will make a big difference. Amen.

≈

My God, my God, why have you abandoned me? (Ps 22:1)

Do you sometimes feel as if Jesus is far away in heaven and has abandoned you? I know I have. There have been many times that I've cried out to him for help with no apparent results. Not only did my problem remain, but I didn't even feel his presence. Sound familiar?

I've discovered that the best way to deal with this feeling of abandonment is to bring it to prayer. Instead of trying to ignore it or complain to your friends, why not tell Jesus exactly how you feel?

While crossing the Sea of Galilee with Jesus one day (Mk 4:35–41), the disciples encountered a frightening storm and feared for their lives. Even though Jesus was with them in the boat, they felt abandoned because he was asleep. What did they do? They woke him up and even accused him of not caring! Jesus responded by calming the storm.

Feelings aren't facts. You may feel as if Jesus has abandoned you, but he hasn't. He might be sleeping, but he is still with you. Go ahead and wake him up. Tell him exactly how you feel. Jesus might be able to sleep through a storm, but he can't sleep through the cries of his beloved disciples. Let's turn to him now.

Hi, Jesus. Even though it doesn't feel like it, I know that you're with me right now. Sometimes I'm afraid to disturb you, but I'm going to take an example from the frightened apostles and wake you up. They felt alone and helpless while you slept, but they somehow knew that waking you would be a good idea. I've decided to do the same thing. Please wake up and help me to recognize your presence. Amen.

Are not two sparrows sold for a small coin? Yet not one of them falls to the ground without your Father's knowledge. (Mt 10:29)

It's easy to give God the credit for all of the pleasant things we experience in life. Because God is good, it's totally logical to associate him with anything that is pleasant. On the other hand, it's not as easy to explain his involvement with suffering and unpleasant circumstances. If he truly is all-powerful and good, shouldn't he be able to stop bad things from happening?

Unless we're careful, we can mistakenly conclude that God's power is limited or that he's not intimately involved in our daily lives. Fortunately, both of these conclusions are false. Commenting about the sparrows, Jesus gives us an idea of just how involved God is with his creatures. He is totally in control—not just of the big things, but the small things too.

Understanding that God is in control can be extremely comforting, as it helps us to realize that we're in good hands. But that still doesn't explain the existence of evil. How can he be in control if he allows evil to happen? The answer lies in the fact that God is so amazing that he can bring good out of any evil that could ever take place. There is no better example than the Crucifixion of Jesus.

It may not feel like it, but your Heavenly Father is aware of every aspect of your life. Furthermore, he is totally in control. In case you forget, remind yourself of what Jesus said about the sparrows. Not only are you never alone, but you are in very good hands.

Dear Jesus, thank you for reminding me that I have a Heavenly Father who is watching over me. Your words help me to remember that my Father doesn't only care about the "big" things but cares about the "small" things as well. With that in mind, I ask you to help me with all of my present challenges. I ask this in your name. Amen.

It was not you who chose me, but I who chose you.
(Jn 15:16)

For a long time I felt that I was the one who sought, and ultimately found, Jesus. In reality, it was the other way around. While I was busy ignoring him for many years, he was constantly seeking me. Why? Because he wanted to be my friend.

If you're feeling lonely and believe that something is missing in your life, take a look at your relationship with Jesus. Being his friend means more than just going to church and keeping the commandments. It's about a personal relationship. He desperately wants to be friends with you. If you've never accepted his offer, do it today.

Tell Jesus you want to be his friend. If you're already walking with him, tell him you want to take your relationship to the next level. Jesus is waiting for you to respond. With him by your side, you'll never be lonely again.

Dear Jesus, it makes me feel really special to know that you deliberately chose me to be your friend. In order for our friendship to grow, however, I need to do some work. I want to know you better and follow where you lead. Please help me and let me know how to proceed. In the meantime, I'll make a point to spend some time with you each day. Thank you for being my friend. Amen.

≈

Jesus was in the stern, asleep on a cushion. (Mk 4:38)

How could Jesus sleep in the middle of a major storm? Was he unaware of the severity of the situation? Did he not care about the frightened apostles? In all likelihood, Jesus was sleeping because he was exhausted. He knew that God was totally in control and wanted the apostles to trust our Heavenly Father as much as he does.

Before they woke up Jesus, the apostles felt as if they were on their own. They couldn't hear Jesus or ask for his help. As a result, they panicked as the storm threatened to sink their boat. Eventually, they grew so desperate that they woke him up.

If you're struggling and wondering why Jesus isn't making his presence known, let the details of this story comfort you. Even though he was silent, Jesus was in the boat and in control of the situation. He's with you too. Instead of panicking, try waking him up.

Dear Jesus, thank you for the reminder of your abiding presence with me. I now realize that you can be present even when I can't see or hear you. This story proves that you do respond to the cries of your frightened disciples. That's me! Please help me to feel the peace that comes from knowing that you're present and in control of my life. The storm I'm facing may be too big for me, but not for you. I'm so glad you're here. Amen.

Before Philip called you, I saw you under the fig tree.
(Jn 1:48)

When Philip told Nathanael that he had found the Messiah, he was met with skepticism. Nevertheless, when Philip persisted and invited his friend to "come and see," Nathanael went with him. Nathanael was shocked when Jesus knew who he was, asking, "How do you know me?" (Jn 1:46–48).

Jesus knows all about you too. He knows your strengths and weaknesses, your likes and dislikes, your desires and fears. And he loves you for who you are—weaknesses and all. In fact, he not only loves you—he *likes* you.

Try to carve out some time today and just sit with Jesus. It would really make him happy!

Dear Jesus, I know that you love me, but it's hard to imagine that you really like me and desire to spend time with me. After all, you're very busy and have millions of people trying to get your attention. I think my problem is that I sometimes forget that you can do all things and aren't bound by the limitations of time and space. You're the ultimate multitasker! I'm so glad you know me and still want to be my friend. Amen.

≈≈≈

And they ridiculed him. (Mk 5:40)

Are you frustrated when people mock your faith or tell you that it's unrealistic to trust in God? Take note of how Jesus responded as he prepared to heal a young girl who was presumed to be dead.

Instead of trying to convince the naysayers with words, he "put them all out[side]" and healed the girl—he got down to business and performed a miracle. Once the girl got up and walked, the people were "utterly astounded" (Mk 5:40–42). I bet they were!

If people laughed at Jesus's ability to perform miracles, they are going to laugh at you when you profess belief in his power. Don't let them take away your hope. "Jesus Christ is the same yesterday, today, and forever" (Heb 13:8), which implies that he can still perform miracles today. This truth is unaffected by your feelings or the criticism of others.

Do you need a miracle in your life right now? Don't be afraid to share your hope and confidence with others. Sure, they may laugh or criticize you, but that's okay. Don't waste your time trying to change their minds with words. Instead, turn to Jesus with confident expectation and ask for what you need. Like the people who laughed at Jesus, they will find themselves "utterly astounded" when he comes through with a miracle.

Dear Jesus, sometimes my faith in you makes me feel alone. When I speak about you and the Church, my friends sometimes laugh or criticize me. My attempts to evangelize have even been met with anger and profanity. I hate to say it, but being your friend isn't always easy. I guess it was tough for you, too, wasn't it? I'm glad that I can always count on your friendship. I know that you'll never desert me. Thank you. Amen.

$$\approx$$

Give me a drink. (Jn 4:7)

When is the last time you saw this verse on a wall plaque or internet meme? Taken out of context, it's easy to ignore. If we take a closer look, however, this verse takes on a whole new meaning. Jesus originally addressed these words to a Samaritan woman two thousand years ago, but they are spoken to us as well.

When initially spoken, this command drew the Samaritan women into a conversation with Jesus, which ultimately led her to believe that he was the Messiah. For us, it's not so much the words that matter, but the fact that Jesus sought out this woman as she went about her daily duty of drawing water at the well. This highly unusual behavior (Jews did not associate with Samaritans) serves as proof that nobody is beyond the reach of Jesus.

Jesus wants to draw you into an encounter with him today. As you read this, remember that he is with you. Then pause and have a brief conversation with him. Say whatever comes to mind, or just spend a few minutes hanging out with him.

Don't worry about coming up with the perfect words. Jesus cares more about your presence than your words.

Dear Jesus, I'm so glad that you're here with me. I'm feeling lonely and could really use a friend. Even though you have millions and millions of friends already, I know that my friendship is important to you. I may not understand it, but I do believe it. Help me always to remember that I matter to you. Thank you. Amen.

Jesus wept. (Jn 11:35)

While the spoken words of Jesus are extremely powerful, it's also important for us to study his *actions*. Why did Jesus weep when he came to the tomb of his newly buried friend? Did he momentarily forget that he had the power to raise Lazarus from the dead? Not exactly.

Jesus wept because he felt for the grieving family and friends of Lazarus. It saddened him to see them suffer. Best of all, his sadness led to action. Jesus did something to relieve their suffering.

Jesus is aware of your tears. If you're crying, he's crying with you and wants to comfort you. If you're lonely, he wants to sit with you and be your friend. Turn to Jesus and ask him to do so. I can't guarantee what he'll do, but I can guarantee that he'll do something to bring you to greater truth and life.

Dear Jesus, sometimes I forget just how human you are. I often view you as an all-powerful miracle worker and forget that you experienced tiredness, hunger, and pain. Even more difficult is remembering that you know what it's like to feel sad. Help me to remember that you often cry with me when I'm crying and grieve with me when I'm grieving. Because you are all-powerful, however, you also have the ability to do something to help me. In your mercy, please grant me the comfort that only you can deliver. I could really use it today. Thank you. Amen.

≈≈

And it happened that while they were conversing and debating, Jesus himself drew near and walked with them, but their eyes were prevented from recognizing him. (Lk 24:15–16)

As the two disciples walked toward Emmaus, they didn't realize that Jesus was walking with them. How many times do we make the same mistake? The fact that you can't see or feel Jesus doesn't mean he isn't present. Rather, it simply means that you can't feel him.

The message is worth repeating: While loneliness can be caused by real situations and be extremely painful, it would be wrong for us to ignore the constant presence of Jesus. We may not hear him, see him, or feel him, but he is present with us at all times.

Jesus was with the two travelers on the road to Emmaus, and he's with you too. He'll reveal his presence in some way when the time is right. You may feel lonely right now, but you are not alone.

Dear Jesus, I find the story of the travelers on the road to Emmaus to be very helpful. It reminds me of the fact that you don't always make your presence known. I don't feel your presence right now, but neither did they. Rather than dwell on how alone I feel, I'll choose to cling to the truth that I am not alone and you are with me right now. Thank you, Jesus. I couldn't ask for a better friend than you. Amen.

≈

Do not be amazed, [then,] brothers, if the world hates you. (1 Jn 3:13)

As Christians, we are called to follow Christ and not the "wisdom" of the world. While you may not experience full-blown hatred, you will probably encounter some degree of ridicule, misunderstanding, or rejection for following Christ. Therefore, as John warns in his letter, don't be amazed when it happens. Furthermore, don't be surprised if this response comes from friends, family, or even your own mind. It probably means you're on the right track.

No doubt about it, the Christian life can be a lonely one at times. In a world filled with materialism and self-centeredness, the message of Jesus is often viewed as unwelcome. As a result, those of us who follow Jesus and embrace his teachings will often be rejected. When that happens, we must make a choice: Jesus or the world.

I'm not saying it's always easy, but we have to choose. If we choose to follow Jesus, we shouldn't be surprised if we experience some degree of loneliness and rejection. Those negative emotions can be lessened or relieved by leaning on the Lord and asking for an outpouring of his grace. I believe it's totally worth it. I hope you do too.

Dear Jesus, I never thought it would be so difficult to be your follower. As I read through the Bible and study your words, however, I'm starting to realize that you never said it would be easy. Ultimately, I will continue to stick with you. Even though it's difficult at times, I believe that you have the words of everlasting life, and I will trust you. Please grant me the grace never to desert you, even when being your disciple causes loneliness and suffering. Keep me faithful to you, Lord. Amen.

6

When You Are Confused

Even if our faith is strong, we will find ourselves confused at times. While it can make us uncomfortable, confusion can help us grow closer to the Lord. Being in the position of not knowing what to do provides us with an opportunity to seek the Lord's assistance and surrender to his will. As is the case with any emotion, however, we can choose how to respond. We can allow the confusion to paralyze us, take matters completely into our own hands, or turn to Jesus and ask him to lead us. In this chapter, we'll view confusion as an opportunity to seek the Lord's guidance and act in accordance with his will. Having that as our goal will guide us in the right direction, even if we encounter some bumps in the road along the way.

I will lead the blind on a way they do not know;
by paths they do not know I will guide them.
I will turn darkness into light before them,
and make crooked ways straight.
These are my promises:
I made them, I will not forsake them. (Is 42:16)

It's difficult to look at this verse and draw the conclusion that the Lord won't come to the assistance of those who need direction. Speaking to the prophet Isaiah, he promises to lead the blind, turn the darkness into light, and turn rough places into level ground. Additionally, he promises to not forsake those who turn to him.

If I heard these words from a trusted friend, I would be filled with peace. Reading them in the Bible, however, can make them feel distant and impersonal—a challenge that can only be overcome by faith. Even though the Church teaches that the Bible contains the inspired word of God, we sometimes struggle to accept that he speaks to us through these special written words.

One of the main reasons I include so many prayers in this book is to help awaken the faith within us and make these messages more believable. That promise to lead the blind and turn darkness into light isn't made by just anyone. It's made by Almighty God. With that in mind, let's turn to God-made-man, Jesus Christ, and ask him to help us truly believe in his words and provide us with the guidance we need.

Dear Jesus, thank you for your willingness to lead me through the darkness. Even though I read your words as spoken to the prophet Isaiah, I'm struggling to truly believe them. I believe them in theory, but putting them into practice as I stumble in the very real confusion and darkness of life is another story. Please grant me the grace to truly believe your words—remove the confusion from my mind and lead me. Thank you, Jesus. I ask this in your name. Amen.

≈

> Those who love me I also love, and those who seek
> me find me. (Prv 8:17)

How well do you know Jesus? Don't panic if this question makes you feel uncomfortable. The truth is that none of us know him as well as we should. Fortunately, however, every day we spend on this earth provides an opportunity to get to know him better.

For many years, I dismissed the phrase "personal relationship with Jesus" as nothing more than fluff. Then one day I hit rock bottom and realized that maybe I needed him. Unfortunately, I didn't know where to find him or how to get to know him. Shortly thereafter, I discovered the secret.

The answer can be found in this Bible verse from the book of Proverbs. If we seek him *diligently*, we will find him. In other words, we will have to do some work in order to find him. If we make a conscious effort to seek the Lord, however, we *will* find him. How do we do that? The main ways are through prayer, reading the Bible, receiving the sacraments, and listening to the Church.

Turn to Jesus and ask him to make his presence known to you today. His answer may come as a thought, a feeling, a smile, a post on social media, or a Bible verse. I don't know how he will answer, but I know he will.

Dear Jesus, searching for ways to know you better can be a confusing process. Some believe that it involves education, saying the right prayers, or retreating from the world, but that sounds way too complicated for me right now. Based on this verse, I should be able to find you if I search for you. I desire to do that today, Lord. Please help me to know you better. I'm willing to work on our relationship, but I need some basic direction first. Thank you for hearing and answering this prayer. Amen.

The Advocate, the holy Spirit that the Father will send in my name—he will teach you everything and remind you of all that [I] told you. (Jn 14:26)

Jesus knew that we would encounter challenging situations in life and didn't want to leave us alone. That's why he made arrangements for the Father to send us the Holy Spirit. While this sending initially happens when we are baptized and is strengthened when we're confirmed, there's something else needed for it to bear good fruit.

The Holy Spirit respects our free will and will not force a way into our lives. Like a birthday present wrapped in pretty paper and decorated with ribbons, the gift of the Holy Spirit needs to be unwrapped before we can enjoy it. It's a good idea to invite the Spirit to come alive in you on a daily basis. Your invitation will give permission for the Spirit to unleash divine power in your life.

If you're confused and trying to do the right thing, call on the Holy Spirit. Ask the Spirit to inspire you to think, speak, and act like Jesus. The Spirit will help you. I know that it sounds too good to be true, but act in faith and do it anyway. Jesus wouldn't make this promise unless it was true.

Dear Jesus, you promised that the Father would send the Holy Spirit to help me remember what you said. I need some help right now. Father God, I ask you in the name of Jesus to send your Spirit to me now. Please awaken the Spirit's power in me, and help me to think, speak, and act like Jesus would in this situation. Thank you. Amen.

≈

Thus says the LORD, your redeemer,
the Holy One of Israel:
I am the LORD, your God,
teaching you how to prevail,
leading you on the way you should go. (Is 48:17)

Before the birth of Jesus, people often viewed God as a distant and frightening ruler. Things began to change, however, when the long-awaited Messiah entered the world as a vulnerable infant. Throughout his public ministry, Jesus not only taught us about God but gave us the ultimate example of how to live our lives.

Even though I'm trying to live my life in a way that pleases God, it's not always easy. Sometimes I don't know what to do or what's truly good for me. Instead of allowing myself to become confused or overwhelmed, however, I will choose to cling to the Lord's promise to show me the way. He created me, knows what's best for me, and is willing to lead me. Why shouldn't I place my trust in him?

Lord Jesus Christ, thank you for your willingness to come into our world. By listening to your words and observing your actions, we learn more about you and discover how we should act. Please open my eyes and heart so I can become more like you in my daily life. Thank you, Lord. Amen.

> All Scripture is inspired by God and is useful for teaching, for refutation, for correction, and for training in righteousness, so that one who belongs to God may be competent, equipped for every good work. (2 Tm 3:16–17)

"God never speaks to me!"

Does this sound familiar? At one time or another, many of us have felt this way. Just because we feel it, however, doesn't make it true. God is constantly speaking to us in many different ways. Unfortunately, we often miss his message because we don't know how to listen. Take a closer look at the above Bible verse. This is God speaking to you now, reminding you that every word contained in the Bible is inspired by the Holy Spirit. Pretty amazing, isn't it?

Do you think the Bible is hard to understand? If so, you're in good company. Referring first to the letters of Paul and then to the rest of scripture, St. Peter wrote, "There are some things hard to understand that the ignorant and unstable distort to their own destruction, just as they do the other scriptures" (2 Pt 3:16).

Don't make the mistake of avoiding the Bible because you feel it's too difficult to understand. Yes, the Bible can be complicated, but that shouldn't stop us. Begin your Bible reading by asking the Holy Spirit to help you understand what you're about to read. Then, instead of dwelling on what you can't understand, focus on what you *can* understand. You don't have to comprehend every word in order to hear the Lord speaking to you through the Bible. Need an example? Jesus is about to speak to you now. Ready?

"Do not let your hearts be troubled" (Jn 14:1).

This is just one example of the extremely personal and relevant messages found in the Bible. If you let him, the Lord will speak to you through his written word. With the help of the Holy Spirit and your openness, he will illuminate your path.

Dear Jesus, even though certain scripture passages are confusing to me, I believe that you can still speak to me through your written word. Please send your Holy Spirit to guide my thoughts and open my heart. I know that many people are guided by the Bible, and I really want to be one of them. Please help me. Amen.

I have told you this while I am with you. The Advocate, the holy Spirit that the Father will send in my name—he will teach you everything and remind you of all that [I] told you. (Jn 14:25–26)

Trying to make an important decision can be very stressful, especially when you don't know what to do. Even the fact that you're trying to do God's will doesn't automatically make you immune to confusion and stress. Knowing how challenging life would be, Jesus didn't abandon us when he ascended into heaven. He sent the Holy Spirit!

For many years I've heard stories of what Jesus said and did, but I sometimes struggle to remember them. It is especially difficult when I find myself in real-life situations and wonder what I should say or do. I often wish that Jesus was sitting next to me, giving me advice. Sometimes I feel so alone and confused.

The fact that you *feel* alone doesn't make it true. You are not alone. Get to know the Holy Spirit. Ask him to guide you. When faced with a difficult decision or challenging situation, he will remind you of what Jesus said and help you know what to say and do.

Dear Jesus, your words and teachings always seem to make sense when I read them in the Bible, but I often struggle to recall them and put them into practice when I need to apply them. You promised that you would send the Holy Spirit to help me with this, and I could really use this help. Please awaken your Spirit in me now so that I'll be prepared for the challenges of this day. Thank you. Amen.

≈

The word of the LORD came to Elijah: Leave here, go east and hide in the Wadi Cherith, east of the Jordan. You shall drink of the wadi, and I have commanded ravens to feed you there. So he left and did as the

Lord had commanded. He left and remained by the
Wadi Cherith, east of the Jordan. (1 Kgs 17:2–5)

Elijah is a great example of someone who obeyed the Lord, even
when he didn't know all the details. In the midst of a serious
drought, the prophet was instructed by God to hide by a brook.
He was told that the brook would be his water supply and the
ravens would provide him food.

No big deal, right? Wrong! It's a huge deal because nothing
about this plan makes sense. Not only were ravens considered
unclean, but they were scavengers. If one was going to choose a
bird to act as a food delivery service, a raven would be near the
bottom of the list. And a brook as a source of drinking water?
Guess what happens to a brook in a drought?

But Elijah obeyed, and God delivered on his promise:
"Ravens brought him bread and meat in the morning, and
bread and meat in the evening, and he drank from the wadi"
(1 Kgs 17:6).

Sometimes God asks us to do some "crazy" things or to
endure unimaginable suffering. How do you typically respond?
Do you trust God like Elijah, or do you run the other way?
Unless you're willing to cooperate with the Lord's plan, you'll
never get to see the miracles he can work in your life. God
wants to provide for your needs and do great things through
you, but you have to go along with his plan. Elijah did just that.
Are you willing to follow his lead?

*Dear Jesus, I know you don't want me to be irresponsible or
impulsive, but I do believe you want me to trust you more. When*

I perceive any potential danger in a particular course of action, even a remote one, I sometimes play it safe and do nothing. Behaving in this manner often stifles your ability to work powerfully through me and prevents me from growing in faith. I ask you for the grace to obey like Elijah, even if I can't be certain of the consequences. Help me to trust you more, Lord. Amen.

> But the LORD said to Samuel: Do not judge from his appearance or from his lofty stature, because I have rejected him. God does not see as a mortal, who sees the appearance. The LORD looks into the heart.
> (1 Sm 16:7)

When looking for a new king to replace Saul, Samuel glanced at Eliab and thought he found his man. The Lord thought otherwise, however, and reminded the prophet that looks can be deceiving. Ultimately, God led Samuel to select David. He was the youngest son of Jesse and worked in the fields as a shepherd, but he was the man God chose to lead his people.

When we look at a person or a situation, we see the outside. God, on the other hand, can see the inside. He can see the potential in that person we just rejected or the danger in that bad decision we're about to make. That's why it's so important to imitate Samuel and seek the Lord's counsel when making decisions. Don't worry. He'll let you know what you should do. Ask for his assistance, and do what you think is best. Even if you make the "wrong" decision, he can make it work out for the best.

Lord Jesus, help me to recognize the fact that my vision is limited. Unlike you, I view my circumstances and choices in a very limited way. Your wisdom is so much greater than mine, and I could use your assistance. Guide my thoughts to the right course of action, and grant me the grace to follow your lead. I ask this in your name. Amen.

≈≈

Follow me. (Jn 1:43)

Every day, you and I have the opportunity to follow Jesus. Sometimes it may require you to make a conscious decision, but many times it simply involves dealing with the events of your daily life. Today you are going to meet various people and experience a unique set of circumstances. The Lord is totally in control of the people and events that make up your day; he exercises his control by either willing or allowing various events and individuals to be a part of your life.

The Lord is in control of everything that happens to you today. He is leading you. Make an attempt to be aware of his presence, and look for ways to serve him in the circumstances he places you in. The people you meet and the situations you encounter are not accidental. You are where you are for a reason. Ask Jesus to use you as his instrument. Ask him to give you the words and guide your steps. He will.

Dear Jesus, it's not always easy to see your hand in the daily events of my life. Sometimes it seems as if things "just happen," but I don't really believe that's true. I recognize that you, as my

Lord, are totally in control of my life, the world, and the universe. Please lead me where you desire me to be today. I believe that you will. In addition, let me know how I can be your instrument in the situations I encounter today. Thank you. Amen.

I am the light of the world. Whoever follows me will not walk in darkness, but will have the light of life. (Jn 8:12)

Make no mistake about it—the world can be a dark place. Even the briefest glance at your social media feed can be enough to spoil your day. Before you know it, you find yourself discouraged or hopeless. Is that just the way it is, or can you do something about it?

Jesus gives us the answer in this verse. He is the light of the world. If we follow him, we won't walk in darkness. Note that he never said that darkness doesn't exist. It does. What he said is that following him allows us to walk in the light, even when we're surrounded by darkness.

If you're reading this, you're on the right track. Instead of being reminded of all the hatred and division in the world, you're thinking about the words of Jesus and what he's saying to you. If you want to start your day off right, try reading some scripture or beginning your day with a few minutes of prayer. You may not be able to make all the darkness go away, but you can make sure that you're walking in the light.

Dear Jesus, I'm surrounded by darkness, and I need you to be my light today. You never promised to remove all the darkness in this fallen world, but you did promise to remain with me and assist me. I'm holding you to your promise, Lord. I can't do it without you. Please shine your light on the road in front of me, illuminate my path, and guide my steps. Thank you, Jesus. Amen.

~~~

> [John the Baptist] was a burning and shining lamp,
> and for a while you were content to rejoice in his light.
> But I have testimony greater than John's. (Jn 5:35–36)

Because John the Baptist had an attractive and hope-filled message, it's easy to see why his disciples were content with following him. Once Jesus came on the scene, however, John's ministry became obsolete, and his followers were encouraged to move on.

It's easy to become content in our relationship with Jesus, but it's generally not a good idea. Even though I like to be totally in control of my spiritual journey, I recognize that it's better to yield to the Holy Spirit. The Spirit knows what I need better than I do. From this moment on, I invite you to be more accepting of those unexpected interruptions and lack of spiritual progress. In order to grow closer to Jesus, we must be willing to move beyond contentment and allow ourselves to be led by his Spirit.

Dear Jesus, from now on, I ask that you lead me to where I need to be. Like John's disciples, I must be willing to move away from contentment and move closer to you. I know it won't always be easy, so please grant me the grace I need and the courage to follow your lead. Thank you. Amen.

~~

For this is the will of my Father, that everyone who sees the Son and believes in him may have eternal life, and I shall raise him [on] the last day. (Jn 6:40)

In this verse, Jesus clearly makes known God's will for you and me. He wants us to believe in him and live with him forever in heaven. Sounds good, but how do we know how to respond?

Believing in Jesus means a lot more than believing that he walked the face of the earth two thousand years ago. If we truly believe in Jesus, we should be willing to listen to his words and do what he commands through scripture and his Church. Simple, right?

It may be simple, but it's not always easy. If you're like me and find yourself struggling to understand what Jesus is asking of us, keep your eye on the prize. Eternal life in heaven with no problems, illness, or suffering is worth the struggle. Keep following Jesus, and you'll get there. He doesn't give us a set of instructions—he gives us something better: his very self. He is the Way, and if we cling to him, he will bring us to the Father.

Dear Jesus, sometimes I don't understand what you're asking me to do. You ask me to love my enemies and follow the teachings of your Church, but it's not always easy to understand what that means in my day-to-day living. I guess that's what faith is all about, right? You know exactly what I need to get to heaven. Please grant me the grace to obey you always, even when I don't understand. Amen.

7

When You Are Suffering

When suffering comes into our lives, it can either lead us closer to God and his peace, or it can drive us away from him and result in discouragement or hopelessness. Ultimately, our response is what makes the difference. Even though it may not feel like it, suffering can be a great blessing and yield many graces. The verses, reflections, and prayers in this chapter are designed to restore hope in the midst of suffering. As the words of Jesus and the teaching of the Church clearly state, it is a totally realistic and achievable goal.

> Jesus, aware at once that power had gone out from him, turned around in the crowd and asked, "Who has touched my clothes?" (Mk 5:30)

How powerful is an encounter with Jesus? Consider the case of the woman suffering from a hemorrhage (Mk 5:25–34). For twelve years she suffered from this ailment, spent all that she had, consulted numerous doctors, and after all that was no better "but only grew worse" (Mk 5:26). Wow. How would you feel if you were in her shoes?

Instead of giving in to despair, however, the woman sought out Jesus. Having heard about him, she believed that simply touching his garments would make her well. And when the opportunity presented itself, that's exactly what she did. Approaching Jesus from behind, she touched his garment and "immediately her flow of blood dried up"!

While the obvious moral of the story is that an encounter with Jesus (no matter how brief) can be life-changing, what really astonishes me is what took place next. Even though he was surrounded by a large crowd of people, Jesus was able to sense the presence of a desperate woman who approached him from behind and simply touched his clothes.

Jesus knows you and loves you. He cares about all of your problems and can help you with them. Don't be afraid to approach him. Instead of giving in to despair, make a point to touch the hem of his garment today.

Dear Jesus, it's hard to comprehend how much you love me. Even though millions of people are reaching out to you every day, you will always make time for me when I approach you. Thank you, Lord. My suffering is great today and I'm not capable of doing much, but I am doing what I can. Just like the woman with the hemorrhage, I desire to touch the hem of your garment. I know that I can do so without even leaving my home. Please grant me the healing I need and restore my hope. Amen.

Jesus entered the house of Peter, and saw his moth-er-in-law lying in bed with a fever. He touched her

hand, the fever left her, and she rose and waited on
him. (Mt 8:14–15)

If you're in need of a healing (spiritual, physical, emotional),
these words should bring you comfort. As I see it, there are five
important lessons we can learn from this story.

1. We don't have to travel far to seek healing from Jesus.
He entered Peter's house and wants to enter your house too.
All you have to do is open the door when you hear him knock.

2. As soon as Jesus entered the house, he saw that Peter's
mother-in-law was sick and healed her. He sees your suffering
and wants to heal you too.

3. The touch of Jesus is all it takes to be healed. Let him
touch your hand and heal you.

4. Once she was healed, Peter's mother-in-law got up and
served Jesus. She didn't waste time wondering if the healing
was legitimate or if she would have a relapse. She got up and
served him. When Jesus heals us, he expects us to use our
transformation to further his work of loving service.

5. Jesus wants to heal us from our physical, spiritual, and
emotional infirmities. Don't feel bad asking him to heal you.

The gospels are filled with stories of miraculous healings
granted by Jesus. Over the course of my life, I have personally
witnessed it many times. I don't know the specifics of how or
when Jesus will heal you, but I do know that he wants you to
ask. Do it today!

*Dear Jesus, the many stories of healing in the Bible give me hope.
I believe that you can heal me. I also believe that you know the*

type of healing I truly need—body, mind, or spirit. I ask for all three and trust that you will give me the healing I need. When my request is granted and I am healed in some way, I promise to repay your goodness by serving others. I know that is what you desire. Thank you. Amen.

A leper came to him [and kneeling down] begged him and said, "If you wish, you can make me clean." (Mk 1:40)

When the soon-to-be-healed leper knelt down before Jesus, he fully believed that Jesus had the power to heal him. He didn't necessarily know that he *would* heal him, but he knew that he *could* heal him.

What is your greatest need or burden right now? Do you believe that Jesus can fix it? Whether you "feel it" or not, kneel before Jesus today and ask him to handle your problem. No matter how you feel, choosing to give your problem to Jesus shows that you believe in his power. It's an example of putting your faith into practice.

I don't know how Jesus will respond to your request, but I know that he will. Be persistent, but trust in his timing. Sometimes he will allow your suffering to continue (at least temporarily) for reasons known only to him. What matters most is that you believe in the power of Jesus and turn to him for help. That's exactly what the leper did.

Dear Jesus, I believe that you have the power to remove my suffering. The many examples of your healing power in the Bible reveal to us that you were sent to restore us to fullness of life, even in the here and now. Though I may not feel it in this moment, I believe it. Please heal me, Jesus. I know that you can. If for some reason you choose to delay my healing, I will trust you. I know that you want what's best for me. Amen.

≈

For you know the gracious act of our Lord Jesus Christ, that for your sake he became poor although he was rich, so that by his poverty you might become rich. (2 Cor 8:9)

In his Letter to the Philippians, St. Paul wrote that Jesus "humbled himself, becoming obedient to death" (2:8). It's an astonishing step, done out of love for you and me. While it was humiliating, uncomfortable, and painful for Jesus, it was the Father's will.

If you are suffering now, God is allowing it to happen for a reason. He would not permit you to suffer if he couldn't bring good out of it. You may not have control over the pain you experience, but you can always control how you respond. You can waste your suffering by lashing out and complaining, or you can embrace your cross and pray for the grace to endure. By doing the latter, you will be connecting your suffering to Jesus's suffering and assisting him in redeeming the world.

St. Paul understood this so deeply that he was actually able to rejoice in his suffering, knowing that it provided an opportunity to save souls: "Now I rejoice in my sufferings for your sake," he wrote, "and in my flesh I am filling up what is lacking in the afflictions of Christ on behalf of his body, which is the church" (Col 1:24).

It seems crazy, but it is possible to rejoice when you suffer. You don't rejoice because suffering feels good, but you choose to rejoice because you are assisting Jesus in his mission of salvation.

Dear Jesus, I have to be honest and tell you that I really dislike the pain caused by my suffering. I'm sure you can relate. You know what it's like to feel pain, and I know you didn't enjoy it either. Because of your desire to do the Father's will and your great love for me, however, you embraced your suffering and allowed it to bear much fruit. I want to do the same thing, but I need your help. I don't want to waste my suffering, Jesus. Please grant me the grace to endure it while I have it. I unite my suffering with yours. Please use it for good. Amen.

There is an appointed time for everything, and a time for every affair under the heavens. (Eccl 3:1)

Suffering can be painful, but suffering with no end in sight can be excruciating. This verse from Ecclesiastes reminds us that, no matter how we feel, no earthly suffering is permanent.

The fact that you *feel* your suffering will never end doesn't make it true. Feelings aren't facts. Job proclaimed with confidence that he would never see happiness again (Jb 7:7), but he was wrong. If you need reassurance, read chapter 42 of the book of Job to see how his story turned out.

Don't allow your feelings to overtake your faith. No suffering—even what Jesus endured on the Cross—will last forever. No matter how painful and hopeless your situation feels, it could be gone tomorrow. Even if it lasts for the rest of your earthly life, the Lord can give you the grace to find peace in the midst of it. Keep praying and believing. God's mercy is bigger than any temporary suffering we will ever be asked to endure.

Dear Jesus, it's tough to find courage in my current situation because it feels so hopeless. I know that my suffering will not last forever, but I'm having a hard time believing it. I'm also having a difficult time believing that I can find peace in the middle of this suffering. Nevertheless, I'm going to choose to place my trust in you, Lord. Please take away my suffering or grant me the grace to deal with it. I know you can do all things. Jesus, I trust in you. Amen.

Everyone who listens to these words of mine and acts on them will be like a wise man who built his house on rock. The rain fell, the floods came, and the winds blew and buffeted the house. But it did not collapse; it had been set solidly on rock. And everyone who listens to these words of mine but does not act on them will be like a fool who built his house on sand. The rain fell, the floods came, and the winds blew and buffeted the house. And it collapsed and was completely ruined. (Mt 7:24–27)

It's hard to misinterpret what Jesus is saying in this Bible passage. It really boils down to three things:

1. We *will* have storms in life.

2. If we listen to Jesus's words and act on them, we will be able to withstand the storms.

3. If we ignore his words, we will fall apart.

Jesus said many things, but let's start with one of my favorites: "Do not worry about tomorrow; tomorrow will take care of itself" (Mt 6:34). Note that he didn't say, "I hope you don't worry," or "Try not to worry." He gave us a command: "*Do not* worry about tomorrow." That implies that we have some degree of control over our anxiety about what might happen tomorrow. And we do.

How will you respond to this command from Jesus? You can either ignore it or obey it. You can worry, or you can pray. There are two choices—it's your decision. Choose wisely!

Dear Jesus, things are not looking good for me right now, and I'm afraid to face the future. I've gotten so used to worrying that it's become a habit. As soon as I'm faced with a problem, I let my mind spin out of control, and I assume the worst. You told me to listen to your words, so I'm choosing to do that right now. Instead of worrying, I am going to think about some of the miracles you performed while you were on earth. If you did it then, I believe you can do it now. I surrender my past, present, and future to you. Please calm my mind and grant me peace. Amen.

≈≈

Consider it all joy . . . when you encounter various trials, for you know that the testing of your faith produces perseverance. (Jas 1:2–3)

Because God is all-powerful, he could prevent us from going through trials. One of the reasons he allows us to go through them, however, is to strengthen our faith. Since our relationship with him depends on faith, it allows us to grow closer to him. Ultimately, he allows these difficulties because he loves us and wants to help us reach for him and place our lives in his hands.

This reflection isn't about feelings. Trials don't usually make you *feel* good. Rather, it's a statement of fact: Trials can help our faith to grow. It may not feel like it, but that's a good thing. God loves us and wants to help us grow closer to him in this life and live with him forever in the next life.

For this reason, James instructs us to "consider it all joy" when we encounter trials and sufferings. He doesn't tell us we have to feel good about them. He tells us to rejoice because they're good for us. It's a hard concept to embrace, but one that can bring a lot of peace if we choose to accept it. Start by believing it in your head. In time, it will flow down to your heart.

Dear Jesus, even though the message of rejoicing over suffering appears multiple times in the New Testament, it's still not easy to accept. I'm used to rejoicing when pleasant things happen in my life. The idea of rejoicing during suffering seems illogical to me. I guess it all boils down to accepting the fact that you know what's best for me. I realize I can choose to rejoice, even if I don't feel like it. I will do that, Lord. I choose to believe that you're allowing me to suffer because you can bring good out of it. While I'm at it, I'll also choose to rejoice for the same reason. I feel a little better now. Thanks for helping me, Jesus. Amen.

> For whoever wishes to save his life will lose it, but whoever loses his life for my sake and that of the gospel will save it. (Mk 8:35)

Those of us who tend to be worriers like to be in control. When we worry, we are trying to find a way to control things that are beyond our control. Following Christ, on the other hand, requires us to give up control and let him take over.

Many of us struggle with the desire to "save our lives" by trying to remain in control, even when it's not possible. Recognizing that it's a common problem, Jesus reminds us that following him is the only way to experience lasting peace in this life and eternal life in the next.

Don't be afraid of the cross. Everyone will experience suffering in life, not just Christians. As followers of Jesus, however, we have the promise of peace even in the midst of suffering. Take it from me—trying to run away from suffering only makes it worse. On the other hand, embracing your cross and following Jesus will give you the peace you seek.

Dear Jesus, it makes me uncomfortable to say this, but I'll say it anyway: I don't like suffering. If I could avoid it, I would. When

I listen to your words, however, I realize that suffering can be beneficial. By offering up my suffering and uniting it with yours, I can actually help myself and others. Because I'm so focused on the things of this world, however, it's difficult to appreciate the long-term benefit of suffering. Please help me move beyond my fear of suffering and increase my desire to embrace my cross. Thank you, Lord. Amen.

≈

Then Peter said to Jesus in reply, "Rabbi, it is good that we are here! Let us make three tents: one for you, one for Moses, and one for Elijah." (Mk 9:5)

In order to give them a boost, Jesus took Peter, James, and John to the top of a mountain and gave them a glimpse of heaven. The sight of Jesus conversing with Moses and Elijah was so appealing that Peter didn't want to leave. At some point, however, Jesus led them back down the mountain and toward Jerusalem where he would be crucified.

As Christians, we're going to have days at the top of the mountain and days down in the valley. No matter where we are, however, we can count on the presence of Jesus. If he chooses to lead you down from the mountain, don't fight it. Follow him. You'll find greater peace carrying your cross with Jesus than by trying to stay on the mountain without him.

Dear Jesus, I can definitely relate to Peter! When I'm on the mountain and my problems are few, I don't want to leave. When I'm suffering in the valley, however, I can't wait to escape. While

I can definitely learn an important lesson from the story of the Transfiguration, it's not exactly one I'm eager to learn. Please inspire my thoughts and help me think more like you. Help me understand that life has both mountains and valleys and that you are with me in both locations. Increase my desire to follow where you lead, and grant me your supernatural peace. Amen.

≈

Peter said to him in reply, "Lord, if it is you, command me to come to you on the water." He said, "Come." (Mt 14:28–29)

Make no mistake, Jesus is capable of eliminating any problem we could ever face. He can easily heal illness, restore finances, or mend broken relationships. Sometimes that's exactly what he does. There are times, however, when he allows the storm and its suffering to remain.

Instead of immediately calming the waves and wind, Jesus invited Peter to come to him in the storm. He may be extending the same invitation to you right now. You may not be able to control the storm, but you can control how you respond to it. Moving toward Jesus is always a good idea.

Even though being in the storm may be uncomfortable, he would not allow you to be there if it couldn't help you in some way. Make an effort to remember that Jesus is with you and will not leave your side. The safety of the boat may look attractive, but the Lord isn't there at this time. He's with you in the storm. Not only are you right where you should be at this moment, but you're in the safest place possible.

Dear Jesus, as I attempt to walk by faith and not by sight, I choose to believe that I'm right where you need me to be at this moment in time. I also choose to believe that you are with me and will help me to find peace in my suffering. Please continue to sustain me and give me the strength I need to remain hopeful. Thank you, Jesus. Amen.

≈

This illness is not to end in death, but is for the glory of God, that the Son of God may be glorified through it. (Jn 11:4)

This is how Jesus responded when he heard that Lazarus was ill. If you know the story, you may question the Lord's choice of words. Didn't Lazarus end up dying from his sickness? He did, but Jesus never said he wouldn't die. What he said is that this sickness wouldn't end in death.

Sometimes the Lord allows our circumstances to get pretty bad. It can even appear that things are hopeless and that there's no way out. Take comfort in the story of Lazarus. The people wanted a healing, but Jesus wanted to give them a *resurrection*. In order to do that, however, he needed a corpse.

Don't lose hope. Place your trust in Jesus and his perfect timing. Just like with Lazarus, sometimes things have to get really bad before they get better.

Dear Jesus, sometimes I get so caught up in my own desires that I can't see the big picture. To be honest, I'm not really sure I want to see the big picture right now. My suffering is so great

that what I want is relief. The story of Lazarus gives me hope
that you are fully capable of doing something even greater than
just solving my problem. I'm clinging to that hope now, Lord.
Things are not looking good, and I'm tired of suffering. Please
come to my assistance and restore my hope. I desperately need
to feel you near me right now. Amen.

> He will wipe every tear from their eyes, and there shall
> be no more death or mourning, wailing, or pain, [for]
> the old order has passed away. (Rv 21:4)

All suffering is temporary. Whatever is causing you pain will be
gone one day—either in this life or in the next. Keeping that in
mind should make your burden a little lighter. In the meantime,
take Paul's advice and unite your temporary suffering with the
suffering of Christ, allowing him to use it for good (Col 1:24).

Your suffering may appear unending, but it is not. It will
end one day, maybe as soon as tomorrow. Move forward with
hope, knowing that the Lord is with you. Unlike your present
circumstances, he never changes and will never leave you.

Dear Jesus, as bad as my current suffering is, I find relief in
knowing that it will not last forever. Please stay with me and
grant me the grace to find peace in the middle of my storm. I
know that you love me, and I will trust in your perfect timing.
Thank you, Jesus. Amen.

8

When You Feel Hopeless

Nothing can be as damaging to our relationship with God as hopelessness. When we feel hopeless, we view our problems as unsolvable and God as someone who is unwilling or unable to help us. Typically beginning with discouragement, the feeling of hopelessness can overtake us in a relatively short time and even lead to despair. Unless we find a way to recognize God's love for us and his power over our difficulties, we will live our days burdened by darkness. The good news lies in the truth that God does love us and can do all things. Nothing is hopeless in his eyes. To find the light he has to offer, though, we have to do some work to train our minds. Let us reflect on God's promises as revealed in the Bible verses and pray for an outpouring of his grace.

> The Lord replied, "If you have faith the size of a mustard seed, you would say to [this] mulberry tree, 'Be uprooted and planted in the sea,' and it would obey you." (Lk 17:6)

Do you sometimes wish your faith was stronger? That's definitely not a bad thing. Having the desire for deeper faith is an important first step, but it's not enough. In addition to having this desire and praying for a stronger faith, Jesus reminds us that we should also make it a point to *use* what little faith we have.

Faith is a gift, but it can be developed. By presenting our needs to God, no matter how we feel, we give him the chance to work in our lives. Ultimately, this will help our faith to grow.

You may be feeling hopeless today, but don't let it stop you from turning to Jesus in prayer. Ask him for the miracle you need. Remind him of his words about the mustard seed. Above all, be patient. We never know if God will show up in our lives in small ways, like a mustard seed sprouting, or in dramatic ways, like trees being uprooted and planted in the sea!

Dear Jesus, I want to believe in your power, but I'm a little anxious. As you know, I have what appears to be an unsolvable problem on my hands, and I'm not sure you can help me. Even though there are many stories of your miraculous works in the New Testament, my situation feels different. Nonetheless, I'm going to give you a chance and ask you to help me. I believe that you hear this and will answer me in some way. Please grant me the grace to trust in your timing and not panic if you don't answer immediately. Amen.

≈

What is your opinion? A man had two sons. He came to the first and said, "Son, go out and work in the vineyard today." He said in reply, "I will not," but afterwards he changed his mind and went. The man came to the other son and gave the same order. He said in reply, "Yes, sir," but did not go. Which of the two did his father's will? (Mt 21:28–31)

What do you think Jesus is trying to tell us in this parable? At first glance, it almost appears as though he's teaching that actions are more important than words. While in some cases that could be true, I don't think that's the main lesson here. I believe the key takeaway comes down to one word: repentance.

Repentance is a key theme in the gospels, and it refers to an internal change or conversion. Sometimes we think of it as a one-time major event that takes place when we decide to follow Jesus. That's only partly true. As followers of Jesus Christ, we're called to some degree of repentance every day.

The first son initially refused to do his father's will, but then changed his mind and did the right thing. The second son either had a change of heart or never meant what he said in the first place. I can relate to both situations. Sometimes I have been the first son, and other times I have been the second. What I've learned is that the Lord's mercy is much bigger than my failings. I may not be able to correct my past mistakes, but I can learn from them and do the right thing today. If you're reading this, so can you. Don't lose hope.

Dear Jesus, I just made a big mistake, and I don't know what to do. My actions caused serious damage, and I don't think it's fixable. Even though I feel hopeless, I'm going to ask for your assistance. You are my only option, Lord. Please help me fix the mess I created. I'm willing to do what I can, but I definitely need your help. Thank you, Jesus. Amen.

> An evil and unfaithful generation seeks a sign, but no
> sign will be given it except the sign of Jonah. (Mt 16:4)

Those are tough words, but don't be distracted by the harsh tone. It's important to understand that Jesus was responding to the Pharisees and Sadducees who were testing him by demanding a sign from heaven. On the other hand, just because you're not one of the "evil and adulterous" people trying to test Jesus, don't assume there's nothing in his words for you.

Are you facing a difficult problem right now and feeling discouraged or even hopeless? Do you need some proof that God can really perform a miracle in your life? The Bible is filled with examples of desperate people who experienced miraculous solutions and healings. Throughout the Old and New Testaments you will find proof that all things are possible for God.

Just as Jesus pointed his skeptical listeners to the story of Jonah, he directs us to open our Bibles and look to the past. God never lost a battle, and he never deserted his people. There has never been a problem that he couldn't handle. Don't make the mistake of thinking yours will be the first.

Dear Jesus, even though I'm not a biblical scholar, I'm well aware of the numerous miracles you performed during your time on earth. You healed the sick, gave sight to the blind, fed five thousand men with five loaves and two fish, and even raised Lazarus from the dead! Thinking about these true stories gives me hope, but I need something more. I need to believe that you can do the same for me now, two thousand years later. I do believe, Lord; please help my unbelief. Amen.

Jesus said to him, "'If you can!' Everything is possible to one who has faith." (Mk 9:23)

You've heard of the power of positive thinking, but what about the power of *negative* thinking? Let me assure you that it's a real thing. By failing to believe in God's power, you can actually close the opportunity for him to work miracles in your life.

I don't know how God will answer you or how long it will take, but I do know he will answer. I have repeatedly seen what he can do. Don't stop praying for your miracle. Your answer could be just around the corner. As the old saying goes, "The only unanswered prayer is the one you don't pray."

Dear Jesus, I have a big problem, and I'm choosing to cast aside my feelings of hopelessness and turn to you in prayer. Even though I'm not feeling overly confident right now, I choose to believe that you can help me. I don't want to stop praying just because my situation feels hopeless. I'm asking you to fix my problem; but, more importantly, I'm asking you to grow my faith in you. Thank you. Amen.

≈

Think of what is above, not of what is on earth. (Col
3:2)

If you're feeling discouraged today, here's something you need
to know. Every feeling of discouragement or hopelessness
begins with a thought. It may stem from a real situation or it
may be imaginary, but your thoughts influence your feelings.

You were created by God to share his joy. He is all-powerful and loves you with an unconditional love. Furthermore,
God is bigger than any problem you will ever face. I know that
it's not easy at times, but the key to living joyfully is to focus
more on God and less on your problems. Try to do that today.
If you slip up, just try to get your focus back on the Lord and
his promises. The more you do it, the easier it gets.

*Dear Jesus, if I spent as much time reading about your miracles
as I did concocting worst-case scenarios, I'd probably be a lot
more hopeful. I know I can't change the past, but I can change
the present. Please guide my thoughts and fill my mind with
reminders of your numerous miracles. I may not be able to control my feelings, but with your help, I can control my thoughts.
Thank you, Jesus. Amen.*

≈

One of his disciples, Andrew, the brother of Simon
Peter, said to him, "There is a boy here who has five

barley loaves and two fish; but what good are these
for so many?" (Jn 6:8–9)

When faced with a difficult problem, there never seems to be a shortage of people to confirm your feeling of hopelessness. Sometimes this confirmation doesn't even come from another person, but from within your own mind.

Philip and Andrew were so focused on the problem and their lack of resources that they overlooked an obvious solution: Jesus. Ultimately, he came through and miraculously provided the food for the people.

What hopeless situation are you facing today? Give Jesus a chance to get involved and perform a miracle. He has a proven history of coming through when we need him because that's who he is—our Savior.

Dear Jesus, thanks for the reminder. Sometimes I concentrate so much on my inability to solve my problems that I overlook your ability to help me. I need your help, Jesus. Please let me know what you want me to do. I'll just do my best and let you do the rest. Amen.

There was a woman afflicted with hemorrhages for twelve years. She had suffered greatly at the hands of many doctors and had spent all that she had. Yet she was not helped but only grew worse. (Mk 5:25–26)

Try to put yourself in the place of this woman. Before you answer, however, consider one important fact. Because of her condition, she was forbidden from coming in contact with other people. Not only was she sick for twelve years, but she had no money and was considered an outcast. The word that best describes her situation is *hopeless*. According to this gospel narrative, however, that's not at all how she felt.

This woman believed that she could be healed simply by touching the clothes of Jesus. As a result, she seized the opportunity and was healed immediately. What if she gave up and stopped believing after two, five, ten, or eleven years? But she didn't give up—she chose to keep believing in the healing power of Jesus, and it changed her life.

You may feel hopeless about your physical, emotional, or financial situation right now. You may be tempted to give up and believe things will never turn around—but don't! This story is included in the Bible for a reason. The Holy Spirit wants you to know that nothing is impossible for Jesus. Turn to him today, and ask for help. I don't know how he'll intervene, but I know that he'll do something.

Turning to Jesus always makes things better in some way. He may change your circumstances, he may change you internally, he may act immediately, or he may take his time. Leave the details up to him. Your job is to imitate this faith-filled woman from the gospel and turn to Jesus for help. His job is to answer your prayer. He will not ignore you.

Dear Jesus, the story of the desperate woman reminds me that there's no magic formula for getting you to answer my prayer.

Rather, it's simply a matter of turning to you with a sincere heart. I come to you now, believing that you can help me. Thank you, Jesus. Amen.

> Be strong, do not fear!
> Here is your God, he comes with vindication;
> With divine recompense
> he comes to save you. (Is 35:4)

When these words were first written, Jesus Christ had not yet come into the world. Now things are different. The Word became flesh more than two thousand years ago and now lives among us. As a result, we are not alone. Although we may face problems, challenges, and suffering, there is no need to be afraid.

Even though our faith teaches us that Jesus is always with us, life has a way of blinding us to that important truth. We're extremely blessed to be able to open the Bible and be reminded of his constant presence. No matter how alone you may feel right now, never forget that the Lord is with you. Not only is he present, but he wants to help you with your problems. Remembering that fact can lessen or remove any fear you may be experiencing.

Thank you for walking with me, Jesus. Even though I sometimes get frustrated over the state of the world, I am living in this place and time for a reason. Unlike those who waited thousands of years for your arrival, I believe you are alive and with me! Please

take away my hopelessness and help me to become more aware of
your presence. I ask this in your mighty and holy name. Amen.

> Suddenly the angel of the Lord stood by him and a
> light shone in the cell. He tapped Peter on the side
> and awakened him, saying, "Get up quickly." The
> chains fell from his wrists. (Acts 12:7)

Are you tired of being held captive by your anxiety? Do you
sometimes feel that your life is controlled by fear? If so, you
are not alone. Many people are living in self-imposed prisons
and don't even realize they have a way out.

Imprisoned by King Herod, Peter, "secured by double
chains, was sleeping between two soldiers, while outside the
door guards kept watch on the prison" (Acts 12:6). Suddenly,
an angel visited him and instructed him to get up quickly. It
was only after he obeyed that the chains fell from his wrists—
just like that.

The world may be telling you to be afraid, but Jesus is telling you to rise and have no fear. In order for the chains of anxiety to fall from your wrists, you have to be ready to "get up" and
follow Jesus. He is the answer to the peace you seek, but you
must be willing to respond to his invitation. Are you willing?

Dear Jesus, I've heard all the "Be not afraid" messages in the
Bible many times, but it's still so difficult for me to put your
words into practice. Your words make sense when I read them,
but everything changes once problems arise in my life. You know

that I tend to panic when things go wrong. I don't want to, but I still do. I need your help, Lord. Please grant me the grace to choose to obey you, especially in times of crisis. Instead of turning to worry and assuming that everything is hopeless, give me the strength to turn to you instead. I ask this in your mighty name. Amen.

~~

Blessed are those who trust in the LORD; the LORD will be their trust. (Jer 17:7)

Isn't it great that God still speaks to us through the Bible? Otherwise, we could easily forget important concepts like this one.

When I think about these words, I realize how many times I place my trust in the people, circumstances, and things of the world. As this verse reminds me, however, all of my hope and trust should be in the Lord. It's then that I'm truly fortunate or blessed. Placing my trust elsewhere only leads to frustration and disappointment.

Dear Jesus, this is just what I needed to hear today! I sometimes have a tendency of trying to find hope solely in the things of the world. As you know, doing so can be extremely frustrating, as it reminds me of my own limitations and my inability to control the actions of others. Sometimes, I keep waiting for things around me to get better, and I get frustrated when they don't. Hoping and trusting in you, however, has a totally different effect. You are an unchanging and infinite source of hope. Jesus, I place my trust in you. Amen.

≈

> And whatever you ask in my name, I will do, so that
> the Father may be glorified in the Son. (Jn 14:13)

At first glance, it seems that Jesus is promising that we'll get anything we pray for as long as we ask in his name. Speaking from personal experience, I know for a fact that simply adding "in Jesus's name" to the end of my prayer doesn't guarantee I'll get what I want. And that is a good thing. We usually have a lot of clarity about what we want in a given moment, but it's much harder for us to know what we truly need.

When deciding what is good for us, Jesus doesn't simply look at our life on earth. He wants to ensure that we make it to heaven. Therefore, when he states that he will do whatever we ask, he is referring to what is *truly* good for us. That may not sound like a big deal, but it really is. Jesus wants us to have a personal relationship with the Father and depend on him for our needs. Asking in his name not only gives us access to the Father, but allows us to surrender to his will. It's another way of saying, "Thy will be done." Simply put, it's the most effective and humble way to pray.

Dear Jesus, at first glance, it sounds as if you will give me whatever I want, as long as I ask in your name. I realize, however, that there's more to it than that. Even though I think I know what's best for me, I understand that you know best. Help me to appreciate your generous offer, and grant me the humility and desire I need to surrender to the will of our Father. When he says no, help me to accept it with gratitude, trusting that you know best. Amen.

> During the fourth watch of the night, he came toward them, walking on the sea. (Mt 14:25)

The "fourth watch of the night" is the period of time between 3 and 6 a.m. For those of us who tend to worry, those are prime worrying hours. Some Bibles translate this as "shortly before dawn," which brings to mind the saying that "it's always darkest before dawn." No matter how you look at it, this is a very difficult time for the apostles. They're in the middle of the storm, and all they see is darkness.

Then Jesus appears. Instantly, their hopeless situation is miraculously transformed.

If things are looking dark for you right now, take comfort in their story. One minute before Jesus appeared, the situation looked totally dark and hopeless. A moment later, everything changed. Keep praying. Jesus will make his presence known at exactly the right time. It could be very soon. Always remember that every miracle begins with a hopeless situation. Don't give up!

Dear Jesus, even though things are looking hopeless for me right now, I recognize that it could turn around in an instant. At this point in time, I have something in common with the apostles as they waited for Jesus to arrive. They felt hopeless, and so do I. As I recall the details of the storm at sea, I remember that their story is over and it had a happy ending. My story isn't over yet. I will choose to believe that you will come through for me as you did for them. Thank you, Jesus. Amen.

9

When You Are Burdened or Overwhelmed

The problems and challenges of life can definitely cause one to become burdened and even feel overwhelmed. Every day, we encounter situations that appear to be unsolvable. As Christians, we have a way to mitigate that drowning feeling—reaching for Jesus, just as Peter did! He can bring us peace, though it is not automatic and does require effort on our part. In this chapter, we'll work on ways to draw upon a relationship with Jesus to lighten our burden. I know it's what you want when you are feeling overwhelmed—it's also what Jesus wants. He may not always take away our problems, but he will always lighten them and help us carry them—if we let him.

> Rising very early before dawn, he left and went off to a deserted place, where he prayed. (Mk 1:35)

Do you ever struggle to make time for prayer? It's a common problem and one that I've wrestled with for many years. Even though I now make a point to pray every day, there are times when I have so much work to get done that it's difficult to give up control and say, "Lord, this time is dedicated to you."

It's not incidental that the Bible tells us that Jesus deliberately made time for prayer. It's a fact that the Holy Spirit wanted us to know. As Christians, we're called to become more like Jesus every day. Here's a simple way to do that right now: As soon as you finish reading this paragraph, put down the book and spend *one minute* praying to our Heavenly Father. Use your own words or recite the Lord's prayer. What matters most is not the words, but that you deliberately choose to withdraw from whatever you're doing and spend time with God. You can resume reading this once you're finished. Go ahead. I'll wait. See you in one minute.

Finished? Congratulations! For the last sixty seconds you looked just like Jesus, who knew the value of prayer. Time spent with God is never wasted. Taking prayer breaks on a regular basis is a great way to find peace in the middle of a crazy world. It's also a great way to imitate Jesus. Keep up the good work.

Dear Jesus, thank you for setting such a great example for us. When I feel overwhelmed and have much to get done, I have a tendency to jump into action and eliminate "unnecessary" activities. As much as I hate to say it, I have often placed prayer in that category. Your example makes me rethink that approach. Nobody had more to do than you, but you still found time to pray. You were never overly burdened. I want to be like you. Help me to remember the importance of spending time in prayer, especially when I'm busy. Amen.

> Everyone who listens to these words of mine and acts on them will be like a wise man who built his house on rock. The rain fell, the floods came, and the winds blew and buffeted the house. But it did not collapse; it had been set solidly on rock. (Mt 7:24–25)

Do you ever panic when an unexpected crisis arises? As a "recovering" panicker (some days are better than others), I can personally vouch for the advice that Jesus is giving. If we listen to his words and put them into practice, we will be less likely to panic when things go wrong. I recommend that you concentrate today on just one of the many important messages of Jesus: "Come to me, all you who labor and are burdened, and I will give you rest" (Mt 11:28).

Instead of losing sleep or worrying about that problem you're facing, take Jesus up on his offer and run into his arms. If you're not sure how to do it, try using very simple words, such as the prayer below.

Here I am, Jesus. I am weary and burdened. Please give me the rest you promised. Amen.

> Those who are well do not need a physician, but the
> sick do. I did not come to call the righteous but sin-
> ners. (Mk 2:17)

With all that's taking place in the world right now, it's easy to
give in to worry, discouragement, or even hopelessness. I'd
like to tell you that I never lapse into that way of thinking,
but that wouldn't be true. Even though I know better, I still
stumble at times.

If you find yourself stuck in a rut and burdened by the
struggles of life, take comfort in the words of Jesus. He came
into our world to give us peace and hope. He came to heal us
from anxiety, fear, and discouragement. In order to be healed,
however, we first need to admit that we're sick. Then we have
to acknowledge that he can heal us—and ask him to do so.

*Lord Jesus, I know you don't want me to find life burdensome.
You want me to look forward to the future with hope and not
dread. I am sick and need your healing touch. Please heal me
and give me your supernatural peace. Thank you. Amen.*

> He said to them, "Come away by yourselves to a
> deserted place and rest a while." (Mk 6:31)

After the apostles returned from ministering to the people,
Jesus invited them to go with him to a deserted place and "rest
a while." Even though there was still much work to be done,

he knew that they needed time alone with him to recharge their batteries.

He makes that same invitation to us today. Make a point to take a break from all of the busyness and stress in your life—go to a quiet place and spend a few minutes with the Lord. If you don't know what to say, simply repeat the name "Jesus" and recognize that you are in his presence. Feel free to read from scripture or speak to him if you wish, but what really matters is that you spend time with him.

Don't let the fact that it sounds so simple fool you. If you need peace, simply spending time with Jesus is the most effective thing you can do. Why? It works not because of anything you say or do. It works because Jesus is real and wants to help you. Let him.

Dear Jesus, even though I can't see you right now, I believe that you are with me. I may not be able to verify it with my senses, but I know it by faith. As I focus on this important truth, I can feel myself becoming more peaceful and less overwhelmed because I trust in your power to keep me safe and bring me life. I know that it's not in my imagination. I believe that you are real and that your presence is helping me. Thank you, Jesus. Amen.

Peace I leave with you; my peace I give to you. Not as the world gives do I give it to you. Do not let your hearts be troubled or afraid. (Jn 14:27)

According to the world, we can only be at peace if we have no problems. According to Jesus, however, we can be at peace *even in the midst of* the storm. Jesus wants to give us his supernatural peace. For that reason, he commands us not to let our hearts be troubled or afraid. Note that his command is not a matter of how we feel. It's a conscious choice.

Jesus repeats this message on the day of his Resurrection. He preached it to the frightened apostles who were hiding from the Jewish leaders behind locked doors. Instead of removing the very real threat around them, Jesus chose to give his followers the gift of his peace. No matter how burdened or overwhelmed you are right now, he can do the same for you.

Dear Jesus, thank you for the gift of your peace. Even though I'm afraid and unsettled right now, I choose to follow your command and place my trust in you. I will not let my heart be troubled or afraid. I trust in you, Lord. Please fill my heart with your supernatural peace. Amen.

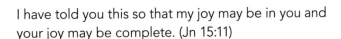

I have told you this so that my joy may be in you and your joy may be complete. (Jn 15:11)

What did Jesus tell us that will bring us complete joy? He told us that he loves us unconditionally: "As the Father loves me, so I also love you" (Jn 15:9).

Don't let the familiarity of these words fool you. This is a really big deal. Nothing you can say or do will make Jesus love you any more or less. No one else will ever love you like that. For that reason, we can choose to rejoice in all circumstances.

Dear Jesus, sometimes I take your love for granted, especially when trying to survive in this crazy world. I'm so busy that I don't have time to think about your unconditional love for me. Instead, I spend most of my time focusing on how I can manage my problems and find some peace. As I examine your words more closely, however, I'm beginning to see that you recommend a different approach. You offer peace and joy that the world cannot give. All you ask is that I follow you and seek your assistance. I'll begin by focusing on your love for me. Help me to better appreciate it, Lord. In the meantime, I'll choose to rejoice because of your unconditional love and your desire to relieve my burdens. Amen.

He woke up, rebuked the wind, and said to the sea, "Quiet! Be still!" The wind ceased and there was great calm. (Mk 4:39)

When the apostles woke Jesus in the middle of the storm, the mere sound of his voice was enough to calm the raging sea. Since "Jesus Christ is the same yesterday, today, and forever" (Heb 13:8), he can calm the storm blowing through your life right now too.

Sometimes Jesus commands the external storm to be still, and other times he calms the internal storm that is raging inside of you. Leave the details to him. His job is to calm the storm that needs to be calmed. Your job is to reach for him and ask for help.

Dear Jesus, when faced with a storm, my first reaction is to do whatever I can to make it go away. If I'm unable to do that, I begin to panic. As time goes on, I become overwhelmed. That's where I'm at right now, Lord. The crashing waves and howling wind are too much for me to handle. Please help me. Even though I'd like you to make the storm go away, I'm going to leave the details up to you. All I ask is that you give me peace. Thank you. Amen.

≈

Then he made the disciples get into the boat and precede him to the other side, while he dismissed the crowds. (Mt 14:22)

After they survived a serious storm on the Sea of Galilee, Jesus made his apostles get back into the boat and head back out to sea. It was the same boat and the same sea, but this time something was different. He wasn't going with them. I find it interesting that they were willing to go, don't you?

The Greek word that Matthew used in the original manuscript (rendered in English as "he made") is *anangkadzo*, which means "to force or compel." Jesus wasn't making a suggestion. He was literally forcing them to get in the boat. Although they had come to understand that Jesus could bail them out if another storm arose, he wasn't going with them this time. That's pretty scary. The apostles definitely learned something during the last storm, but Jesus knew they needed to learn more.

Even though the storms of life can help our faith to grow, very few of us would choose willingly to enter into them. Sometimes Jesus places us in a boat when wind and waves are headed our way. Why? Not because he wants to torture us, but so that we can recognize our own weakness and learn how much we need his help. If you find yourself feeling overwhelmed as you battle a relentless storm, look at it as an opportunity to grow in faith and turn to Jesus. The more you rely on his help, the easier it gets.

Dear Jesus, even though I believe that the storms of life can offer me lessons, I still don't like them. In spite of my feelings, I want to better appreciate and embrace my current and future storms. I need your help with this, however. Please give me the grace to better appreciate the value of these unpleasant experiences. Just like you did with the apostles, I understand that you will make me get into the boat at times. I'm okay with that because I trust that you are ready to help me when I need it. Thank you, Lord, for leading me—I will follow you. Amen.

Rise, take up your mat, and walk. (Jn 5:8)

This seems like an unreasonable thing to say to a man who was unable to walk, but Jesus used this technique often. Whether it's telling the man with a withered hand to stretch out his arm or telling the apostles to feed five thousand men (plus women and children) with five loaves and two fish, Jesus frequently asked people to do what appeared to be impossible.

What impossible task is Jesus asking you to do today? Maybe he's asking you to carry the cross of a painful illness or to forgive someone who has hurt you greatly. Maybe you're being asked to keep praying for an intention that hasn't been answered for months or years. Maybe you're being asked to seek healing from anxiety or a general sense of hopelessness that you've carried your whole life.

Although it may seem like it, Jesus will never ask you to do something impossible. What he's asking might be impossible for you, but not for him. Putting us in these "impossible" situations helps us to realize our limitations and recognize how much we need him.

Dear Jesus, I'm feeling overwhelmed today as I face a problem that seems too big for me to handle. After thinking about the paralytic and the man with the withered hand, however, I see things differently. Even though it seems as if you're asking me to endure something I can't handle, I'm going to choose to trust you. You wouldn't allow me to be in this storm if you didn't think I could handle it. With your help, Lord, we can do this. Please help me. Amen.

≈

The Lord said to her in reply, "Martha, Martha, you are anxious and worried about many things. There is need of only one thing. Mary has chosen the better part and it will not be taken from her." (Lk 10:41–42)

Jesus didn't criticize Martha for working—he criticized her for being "anxious and worried." Unlike her sister, Mary recognized the importance of spending time with Jesus when he came to visit. What would have happened if Martha spent a few minutes with the Lord before she started serving?

A priest once told me that I should never be afraid to "waste time with the Lord," even when I had much work to do. He was right. I can't say for sure that Martha ever learned this lesson, but I learned that spending time with Jesus before jumping into action is a great way to avoid anxiety and worry.

The Lord knows that we have responsibilities, some of which can be stressful. Unless we make time for him, however, our stress will be compounded and we'll end up "anxious and worried" like Martha. Make a point to spend a few minutes with Jesus today and ask for the strength to deal with your daily responsibilities and challenges. Do it especially if you're extremely busy. Time spent with the Lord is never wasted.

Dear Jesus, when am I ever going to learn my lesson and stop trying to do everything on my own? So many times I jump into action and totally forget about asking you to help me. Even though this behavior always results in my becoming overwhelmed and anxious, I continue to do it. I'm determined to change, Lord. Beginning right now, I resolve to spend some time with you before I jump into action. Please help me to remember this when the next crisis comes around. Amen.

≈

> Now since the children share in blood and flesh, he
> likewise shared in them, that through death he might
> destroy the one who has the power of death, that is,
> the devil, and free those who through fear of death
> had been subject to slavery all their life. (Heb 2:14–15)

Do you sometimes feel that you can't break free from the stress and burdens of life? If so, you're not alone. The good news is that we don't have to live this way. Jesus came into our world to free us not only from the slavery of sin but also from excessive fear and hopelessness. With his assistance, we can experience peace even in the midst of trials and tribulations.

Satan wants to keep us enslaved and fill our minds with thoughts of discouragement, hopelessness, and doom. Jesus, on the other hand, proclaims a message of hope and peace. Whom will you listen to today? You can choose to believe the One who loves you, who won the victory on Calvary, or the liar who wants to keep you enslaved to misery and hopelessness.

Dear Jesus, thank you for bringing hope into our fallen world. Though I'm not sure how I'll get through the overwhelming situation I'm in, I know you are here with me, sharing this experience so that you can bring me to fullness of life. When I look to you, I know I can find the hope I need to face this challenge. Please grant me the strength I need to carry this burden, and, furthermore, use me as an instrument of hope to those around me today. With your help, I know this is possible. Amen.

≈

Come to me, all you who labor and are burdened, and I will give you rest. (Mt 11:28)

We've all heard these words so many times that it's easy to ignore them—*don't*! Jesus unconditionally promises rest for those who follow him. That doesn't mean we can escape from suffering and difficulties. We can't. What it does mean is that we can experience peace if we go where Jesus leads.

Even when he leads us down a path filled with difficulties and suffering, his promise remains. When faced with challenges, your peace will only be found in embracing your cross with Jesus by your side. It's a hard concept for us to accept and one that runs contrary to the wisdom of the world, but it's the truth. The peace we all seek can only be found by following Jesus—wherever (and I mean *wherever*) he leads.

Dear Jesus, while the concept of coming to you and finding rest is very attractive, it can also be very confusing. I can see how it applies when things are going well in my life, but I'm struggling to see how it applies when I'm suffering. As I read and reread your words, however, I don't see any disclaimers or qualifications. Therefore, your offer must be valid in all circumstances— whether they are favorable or unfavorable. I'm going to take you at your word. Here I am, Jesus. I am completely overwhelmed and burdened, and I desperately need some relief. Please help me. Amen.

10

When You Are in Need and Feel Helpless

Although the feeling of helplessness can easily lead to despair, it can also serve as a turning point for a closer relationship with God. Many stories of conversion, including my own, begin with the realization that we are helpless and need assistance. The practice of total self-reliance is incompatible with the Christian life because it takes God out of the picture. Failing to recognize our need for God makes it impossible for us to follow him. It may not be comforting to feel helpless, but that feeling will typically fade once we learn to view it as an *invitation*. Realizing that I am helpless can lead me into the arms of Jesus, who wants to assist me.

Jesus did this as the beginning of his signs in Cana in Galilee and so revealed his glory, and his disciples began to believe in him. (Jn 2:11)

The miracle at the wedding at Cana reminds us of the intercessory power of the Blessed Mother. Jesus didn't *need* her to approach him before performing his first miracle, but he *chose*

131

to wait until she did so. Why? Maybe so that we can see what happens when Mary intercedes for those in need.

When Mary saw that the wine had run out, she knew that it would cause the bride and groom to be embarrassed. Fully aware that she couldn't fix the problem, Mary approached the one who could. This is the only recorded incident of Mary asking Jesus to help someone and, based on biblical evidence, it is 100 percent effective!

Think of what you need right now, and ask Mary to bring it to Jesus for you—he doesn't refuse his mother. I can't guarantee that you will see a jaw-dropping miracle, but it's definitely a possibility. How will you know if you don't ask?

Dear Blessed Mother, I'm turning my "impossible" situation over to you with the hope of receiving a Cana-like miracle. I'll leave the details up to you and Jesus, but I could really use your assistance. I know that you will take my request to your Son. Please obtain for me the grace to wait on his timing and to recognize and accept his response so that my faith will grow stronger. Amen.

≈

I form light and create darkness,
I make well-being and create woe,
I am the LORD, who do all these things. (Is 45:7 RSV2CE)

Nothing can happen in the world or in your life unless God wills it or permits it. He is totally in control. Even when it doesn't seem like it, this statement remains true.

As we journey through life, it's easy to miss the constant presence of God. We are so used to depending on our senses that it becomes difficult to recognize the presence of an unseen, unheard Spirit. Reminders like this one from Isaiah help, and an openness to "seeing" and "hearing" in a new way make it possible. Our senses deceive us when they inform us that we are helpless and alone. With Jesus by our side, both of those notions are totally false.

Dear Jesus, when I look at the messiness of my life, I often struggle to feel your presence. It's even more difficult to see you when I look at what's going on in the world. I guess it's not always about feelings, is it? For that matter, I suppose it's not all about understanding, either. After all, you're God and I'm not. Thanks for the scriptural reminder that you're in control. I will choose to believe it, even if I don't always feel it. Please grant me the grace to trust you more. Amen.

≈

Yes, people of Zion, dwelling in Jerusalem,
you shall no longer weep;
He will be most gracious to you when you cry out;
as soon as he hears he will answer you.
The Lord will give you bread in adversity
and water in affliction. (Is 30:19–20)

As stated in the first verse of this Bible passage, we can be assured that God will always answer us when we turn to him in prayer. Continuing on to the second verse, however, we learn that he promises to give us what we *need*, not necessarily what we want. Sometimes we confuse our needs and wants. How can we tell the difference?

Determining whether our desires fall into the "needs" or "wants" category isn't always easy. In fact, it's often impossible. Our fallen human nature and inability to see with God's perfect vision can render us incapable of determining if something is a need or a want.

Fortunately, there is a way to handle this limitation. When we pray in the Our Father, "Thy will be done," we leave the final decision up to the Lord. Praying like this mirrors the prayer of Jesus and enables us to surrender fully to God's sovereign will. It also makes it unnecessary to determine if we're asking for a "need" or a "want" and allows the Lord to decide. Let's pray for the grace to accept God's wisdom and timing.

Dear Jesus, thank you for reminding me that you always hear and answer my prayers and for supplying all of my needs. Please help me to be more willing to give you the benefit of the doubt when it comes to answering my prayers. I want to trust you, but sometimes it's difficult. Please help me. Amen.

Then Jesus went from that place and withdrew to the region of Tyre and Sidon. And behold, a Canaanite woman of that district came and called out, "Have pity on me, Lord, Son of David! My daughter is tormented by a demon." But he did not say a word in answer to her. (Mt 15:21–23)

Isn't Jesus's response here rather disturbing? This poor woman was begging for mercy, and Jesus didn't even answer her! Was he being mean, or did he have something up his sleeve?

We can get some insight by looking at what happened next. Refusing to give up, the woman persisted in asking for her daughter to be healed. Ultimately, her request was granted, and Jesus praised her great faith!

Don't stop asking Jesus for what you need. As this encounter illustrates, sometimes your request will be met with silence. The Lord often does this to strengthen our faith. Don't assume that his silence means no. Be persistent and keep praying. Jesus hears you, and though it might not come in the form you expect, he will respond.

Dear Jesus, although this example is a little disturbing, it makes me feel better. I can relate to this woman. Right now, I have a pressing need, and you don't seem to be answering. As I look at the details of her story, I see that your silence didn't imply that you didn't care or didn't hear her. It meant that you were testing her faith. I ask you to answer my prayer, but I also ask you for the grace to accept your silence patiently. Thank you. Amen.

As they led him away they took hold of a certain Simon, a Cyrenian, who was coming in from the country; and after laying the cross on him, they made him carry it behind Jesus. (Lk 23:26)

After being scourged, beaten, and crowned with thorns, Jesus was definitely in a weakened state. Between the blood loss and the battering, it would be extremely difficult to walk with a heavy cross. Fearing that he might collapse before reaching the site of his crucifixion, the authorities seized Simon of Cyrene and forced him to help Jesus carry his cross. Doing so would ensure that the public humiliation and execution would proceed as planned.

It's easy to look at this as a case of someone being in the wrong place at the wrong time or simply a matter of happenstance, but I believe it's more than that. While God never wills evil and certainly didn't cause Jesus to be crucified, he allowed it to happen in order to bring about a greater good: the redemption of humanity. With that in mind, we can justifiably say that the Crucifixion was part of God's plan and that the unaware and unwilling Simon played a part in that plan.

Without the assistance of Simon of Cyrene, it's highly likely that Jesus would have collapsed before reaching Calvary, thus threatening his redemptive mission. Simon may not have realized it, but he played a role in the Lord's redeeming work. God used Simon's unwilling assistance to ensure that the weakened Jesus would complete his mission.

In his almighty wisdom, God knows when we need a Simon of Cyrene and will make him available. If you need help carrying your cross right now, ask the Lord to provide a Simon for you. He might come in the form of a spouse, a friend, or a random person you meet in the grocery store, or he might even be Jesus himself. No matter what the case, God will provide in the right way and at the right time.

Dear Jesus, it's difficult to imagine that you needed help, but that was indeed the case as you struggled to carry your heavy cross. Thank you for giving me a great example of humility and trust. Sometimes it's not easy for me to trust in the Father's plan, especially when I realize that I need help. Your example reminds me that it's okay to pray for and accept assistance. Please send me a Simon of Cyrene to help me carry my cross. I will do my part by imitating you and accepting the help when it arrives. I know you won't let me down, Jesus. It's good to know that I don't have to carry my cross alone. Amen.

After some time, however, the wadi ran dry, because no rain had fallen in the land. So the word of the LORD came to him: Arise, go to Zarephath of Sidon and stay there. I have commanded a widow there to feed you. (1 Kgs 17:7–9)

Are you concerned that God's source of provision for you is about to dry up or has dried up? You can find comfort by looking at the life of Elijah. In order to keep the prophet moving forward, God forced him to leave his comfort zone. He will do the same with you.

When God first called Elijah to be a prophet, God instructed him to hide by a *wadi*, or stream. Elijah obeyed, and the Lord held up his end of the bargain. Shortly thereafter, we see a new challenge unfold, as the prophet's source of water dried up. At some point (we don't know how long), God provided a new set of instructions to Elijah. He was told to move to Zarephath, which was pagan territory, and to allow a widow to provide for his material needs. A helpless and dependent widow as a source of provision? In enemy territory? *Seriously, Lord?* Once again, Elijah was called to step out in faith in a *big* way. He obeyed.

God frequently allows "streams" to dry up in our lives so that we don't get too comfortable. Furthermore, there is sometimes a gap between the stream drying up and the revelation of what's next. Don't panic. Everything that happens in your life is designed to increase your faith and draw you closer to God.

If your stream has dried up, keep your eye on the Lord for a new set of directions. It might take a little while, so be patient. God will eventually reveal his plan for you. When he does, follow the example of Elijah and obey his commands. Elijah had no regrets, and neither will you. God will provide for your spiritual and material needs.

Dear Jesus, in the Sermon on the Mount, you assured me that your Father will provide for all of my needs. The story of Elijah is a great example of that. Yet I'm not a prophet, and I don't live in biblical times. Although I believe that your offer applies to me, too, I'm not feeling it. Please supply my need and increase my confidence in you. Amen.

He said to them in reply, "Give them some food yourselves." But they said to him, "Are we to buy two hundred days' wages worth of food and give it to them to eat?" (Mk 6:37)

After a long day of ministering to the crowd, the disciples urged Jesus to wrap it up so that the people could leave and buy themselves something to eat. As he often did, however, Jesus challenged them to do something that was technically impossible. How could they feed five thousand men (plus women and children) when all they had was five loaves and two fish?

Jesus specializes in taking our "not enough" and multiplying it so that it becomes more than enough. I frequently come to the conclusion that I can't love this annoying person, write this book, give this talk, find peace in the midst of suffering, or any number of other "impossibilities." And then I remember to ask Jesus for help.

We've discussed the miracle of the loaves and the fish several times in this book, but there's a particular point I want to highlight here. Even though the apostles didn't think they had enough to feed the people, they had something even more important. They had Jesus, who could transform their shortage into an abundance. He can do the same for you too.

Dear Jesus, this Bible verse reminds me that I may be lacking in some things, but you are always willing to assist me. I'll continue to do my best, but I really need you to multiply the few "loaves and fish" I have to offer. Please come to my assistance and remove my doubts. This story proves that you can always make up for what we lack. Thank you for caring for me so much. Amen.

≈≈

As they were leaving the boat, people immediately recognized him. (Mk 6:54)

We have prayed with the Bible passage that tells of Jesus walking on the water when the apostles were facing the wind and waves. When they were caught in that storm, they were so terrified that they didn't recognize Jesus approaching them.

Then, after they crossed over the lake safely and arrived on the other side, Jesus was immediately recognized by the people there. Isn't it interesting that the crowds recognized Jesus immediately, but those closest to him did not? That's what the storms of life can do—they narrow our focus and prevent us from looking outside of our immediate concerns. If you don't see Jesus right now because your needs feel overwhelming, take a closer look. He's with you.

Dear Jesus, because I can't see you with my eyes or hear the sound of your voice, I often forget that you are alive and always with me. I really need you to become real to me right now, but I can't do it on my own. Please grant me the grace I need to make it happen. Until then, I'll keep having these conversations with you even if I don't feel anything. No matter how I feel, however, I believe in you and will keep making time for you. Even though I have a long way to go, I think I'm on the right track. Amen.

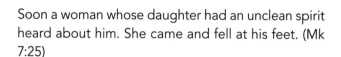

> Soon a woman whose daughter had an unclean spirit
> heard about him. She came and fell at his feet. (Mk
> 7:25)

The fact that this woman fell at the feet of Jesus reveals a great deal about her mindset. Even before she spoke a word, we know that she was desperate and humble. She had a big problem and knew that only Jesus could help her. As a result, this woman was willing to do whatever was necessary to reach out to him.

When her initial request seemed to be rejected by Jesus, she wasn't discouraged. She just humbled herself and asked again. Her faith in Jesus was rewarded, and her daughter was healed.

I don't know what was going on in her mind, but Jesus almost certainly did. Even though she was humble, maybe she needed to become more persistent or trusting. For some reason, Jesus was testing her faith—and she passed with flying colors.

If you need something from the Lord today, keep asking until you get a definitive answer. As this example proves, sometimes he is waiting for you to grow more humble, trusting, or persistent.

Dear Jesus, I wish I could be more like this woman. Not only was she humble, but she was persistent. She knew that you could help her and was not about to give up until you granted her request. Some may call her stubborn, but I look at her as someone with strong faith. Please supply my need and increase my faith, Lord. I don't want to give up on you. Amen.

~~

Then the boy's father cried out, "I do believe, help
my unbelief!" (Mk 9:24)

When a man brought his son to Jesus for healing in Mark's
gospel, he hesitated as he made the request. By using the words
"if you can" (Mk 9:22), the desperate father gave away what he
was thinking. He wasn't entirely convinced that Jesus could
pull this off. Jesus responded by emphasizing that everything
is possible to one who has faith.

Rather than trying to fake it, the man humbly asked Jesus
to strengthen his faith. Obviously, he had *some* faith or he
would never have asked Jesus for help. Nonetheless, he recognized that something was lacking, and he asked Jesus to help
him believe. There's a lesson here for us. No matter how much
we believe, we could all benefit from a faith booster shot. Don't
be afraid to ask Jesus for it.

*Dear Jesus, you often spoke about the importance of faith and cited
it as the reason for prayers being answered, yet I often forget to pray
for an increase in this critical virtue. I get so caught up in my other
needs that I just forget to ask. Not this time, Lord! This man's words
sum up exactly my dilemma. I trust you a little, but I want to trust
you a lot. I believe in you, Jesus. Please help my unbelief. Amen.*

~~

The LORD is my shepherd; there is nothing I lack. (Ps 23:1)

I have often heard that Psalm 23 is the most popular of all the psalms, but I never tried to substantiate that claim. Deciding to finally put it to the test, I did a Google search for "most popular psalm," and Psalm 23 was at the top of every list! What is it about this psalm that makes it so popular?

This psalm, and this verse in particular, assures us that God will provide for all of our needs. Case closed, right? Not exactly. This is a very difficult message to believe. What about all of our unmet needs and unanswered prayers?

I find it best to work backward on this one. According to this verse, God is providing for all of my needs, and I lack nothing. I may not always feel it (many times I don't), but he is giving me what I need. If I don't have it, then I must not need it. Even if he allows me to go through something painful, I may not want it, but I must need it.

I know it's tough to accept, but the Bible is clear on this. God gives us what we need, when we need it. In my opinion, we often focus more on what we don't have than on what we do have. Life is filled with distractions, and we can easily lose sight of the presence of God. Spend some time with him today, and you might realize that many of your wants aren't really that important after all. If you have God in your life, you have all you need.

Dear Jesus, you already know that I struggle to differentiate between my needs and my wants. As I examine the first verse of this popular psalm, however, I'm reminded that in you I already have all I need. With you in my life, I can face the future with confidence. Thank you for coming into the world and walking with me. Because I have you, I am not afraid. If I truly need something in this life, I know that you will make sure I receive it. I am grateful for your providing care for me, Lord. Amen.

> So humble yourselves under the mighty hand of God, that he may exalt you in due time. Cast all your worries upon him because he cares for you. (1 Pt 5:6–7)

Worrying results from trying to control the uncontrollable. It happens when, instead of doing what we can, we also try to do what we can't. When we worry, we are trying to do God's job.

Humility is seeing ourselves as we really are: creatures who are totally dependent on God. He expects us to do what we can, but he also wants us to ask for his help and to recognize that some things are beyond our control. Once we recognize who he is—and who we are—life becomes more peaceful.

Dear Jesus, thank you for letting me realize that I have needs I can't satisfy. While it sometimes makes me uncomfortable, it also helps me to realize how dependent I am on you. That's a good thing, isn't it? I will continue to do my best and turn to you for the rest, as you are capable and willing to help me. Thank you. Amen.

Conclusion

Even though this is my fourteenth published book, writing the conclusion is always a bittersweet experience for me. On one hand, I'm relieved that my deadline has been met and the manuscript is complete. On the other hand, I'm sad that the project is over. Writing a book is a very spiritual experience for me, as it causes me to face my limitations and rely heavily on the Lord.

Speaking of limitations, I'd like to share some behind-the-scenes information with you. A few months ago, my wife, Eileen, had a convulsive seizure while she was sleeping and was diagnosed with epilepsy. A few weeks after that, she was diagnosed with glaucoma and needed emergency eye surgery. Thanks to God and some excellent medical care, she's doing well and living a relatively normal life. That being said, however, this situation has impacted our entire family. I have picked up additional family duties, which must be balanced with my professional responsibilities.

Throughout the process of writing this book, I experienced *doubt*, *uncertainty*, *fear*, *weakness*, *discouragement*, *loneliness*, *confusion*, *suffering*, *hopelessness*, and *helplessness*, and I often felt *overwhelmed* and *burdened*. I don't think it's a coincidence that each of those feelings is covered in this book. I tell you this because I want you to know that I leaned heavily on Jesus throughout the writing process. I needed him to be real to me—not just to help me write the book, but to make it through a challenging time. Not only did I compose the prayers in this book, but I also *prayed them from the heart.*

This book was written by someone who felt every one of the emotions listed in the table of contents. It was written by someone who didn't always sense the Lord's presence. It was written by someone who wondered how he would find the time to complete the manuscript. It was written by someone who watched his wife convulsing and unresponsive on the bed, wondering what life would look like if she didn't survive. It was written by someone who desperately needed Jesus from the Bible to show up and be real to him in the here and now. It was written by someone who is extremely grateful that the Lord did just that.

Even though Jesus is a real person who loves us and is capable of easing our burdens, we can sometimes lose sight of that in the middle of a crisis. I wrote this book to remind you of that fact and to help you connect with him in the middle of the storm. Jesus is real and will help you just as he helped the sinking Peter. No matter how you feel, lean on your faith and give him a chance. He won't let you down. You are in my daily prayers.

Gary Zimak is a Catholic speaker and bestselling author of several books, including *Give Up Worry for Lent!*; *Let Go of Anger and Stress!*; *Give Up Worry for Good!*; *Let Go of Your Fear*; *When Your Days Are Dark, God Is Still Good*; and *Find Peace in Advent!*

Zimak is the host of the *Following the Truth* podcast. He previously served as director of parish services at Mary, Mother of the Redeemer Catholic Church in North Wales, Pennsylvania, and as the host of *Spirit in the Morning* on Holy Spirit Radio in Philadelphia, Pennsylvania. He is a frequent speaker and retreat leader at Catholic parishes and conferences across the country.

His work has appeared in *Catholic Digest, National Catholic Register, Catholic Exchange, Catholic Philly,* and *Catholic Answers Magazine.* Zimak has been a guest on numerous television and radio programs, including *EWTN Bookmark, Seize the Day* with Gus Lloyd, *Women of Grace, Catholic Answers Live, Morning Air,* and the *Son Rise Morning Show.*

Zimak earned a bachelor's degree in business administration from Drexel University.

He lives in Mount Laurel, New Jersey, with his wife. They have two children.

Website: followingthetruth.com
Facebook: Gary.Zimak.speaker.author
X: @gary_zimak

MORE BY
GARY ZIMAK

Give Up Worry for Lent!
40 Days to Finding Peace in Christ

In *Give Up Worry for Lent!*, Gary offers fellow worriers practical, scripture-centered advice on how to relinquish the need to control the uncontrollable—not just for Lent but for good—and how to find peace in Christ.

Give Up Worry for Good!
8 Weeks to Hopeful Living and Lasting Peace

This eight-week resource can be used any time of year and will teach you how to get rid of the stressful, energy-sapping behaviors that keep you on edge and rob you of joy.

Find Peace in Advent!
4 Weeks to Worrying Less at Christmas

Is it really possible to find peace during one of the busiest and stress-filled times of the year? Gary offers a practical, scripture-based approach to Advent so that we can make room for Jesus in our chaotic and fast-paced lives.

Let Go of Anger and Stress!
Be Transformed by the Fruits of the Spirit

Using the nine fruits of the Spirit as a guide, Gary will help you free yourself from anger so that you can find peace and to live the life God has planned for you.

Let Go of Your Fear
Choosing to Trust Jesus in Life's Stormy Times

Gary explores two gospel stories of Jesus calming storms—and his disciples—to show you how to manage the big feelings of fear in your life.

When Your Days Are Dark, God Is Still Good
Biblical Advice to Help You Trust in Difficult Times

In *When Your Days Are Dark, God Is Still Good*, Gary shares personal stories and scripture narratives to show you that God not only is present in your pain but also uses your suffering to transform you into a holier, more compassionate person.